Crete and the Island of Santorini

3rd Edition

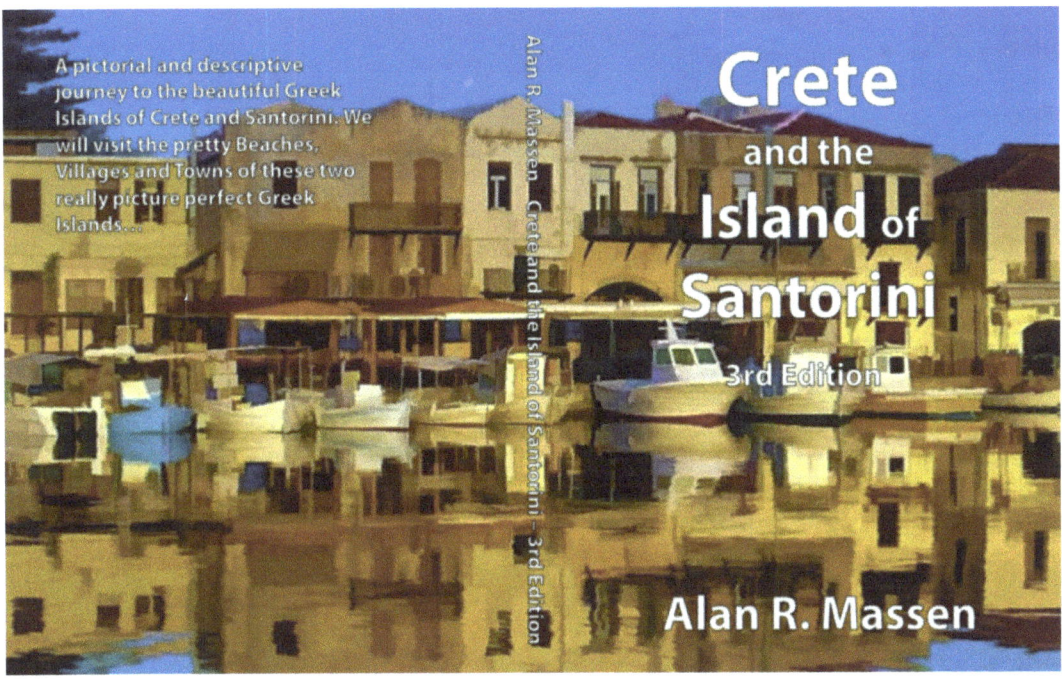

A pictorial and descriptive journey through the history and beauty of the Greek paradise islands of Crete and Santorini that are set in the warm blue Mediterranean Sea. We will explore there history, culture, pretty beaches, villages and towns of these two picture perfect island of Greece.

by Norfolk Watercolour Artist - Alan R. Massen
Published in Great Britain by Rainbow Publications UK

First Published in 2018 by Rainbow Publications UK
2nd Edition Published in 2019 by Rainbow Publications UK
3rd Edition published in 2020 by Rainbow Publications UK

Copyright © 2020 Alan R. Massen

The moral right of Alan R. Massen to be identified as the author of this work has been asserted in accordance with the UK Copyright, Designs and Patents Act of 1988. All rights reserved. No part of this book may be reproduced, or stored in a retrieval system, or transmitted in any form or by any means, electronic, mechanical, photocopying, recording, or otherwise, without the prior written permission of both the author and the above publisher of this book All imagery and illustrations

© Alan R. Massen

Neither the publisher nor the author can accept liability for the use of any of the materials, methods or information recommended in this book or for any consequences arising out of their use, nor can they be held responsible for any errors or omissions that may be found in the text or may occur at a future date as a result of changes in rules, laws or equipment All manufacturers, sellers, product names and services identified in this book are used in editorial fashion and for the benefit of such companies with no intention of any infringement of trademarks. No such use or the use of any trade name is intended to convey endorsement or other affiliation with this book. Every effort has been made to obtain the necessary permissions with reference to copyright material, both illustrative and quoted. We apologize for any omissions in this respect and will be pleased to make the appropriate acknowledgements in any future edition.

Paperback Edition ISBN 978-0-9935591-6-7

Typeset in Minion Pro
Published in Great Britain by Rainbow Publications UK

About the Author

Alan was born in the city of Norwich in the county of Norfolk, England in November 1949. When Alan was still a teenager he started painting whilst attending art classes in Norwich. In his mid-teens he had two paintings accepted for a National Art Exhibition held in London and other major UK cities. Alan spent most of his working life as a professional Health and Safety Advisor and rarely picked up a paint brush until Alan, his wife Susie and daughter Ginny (his other daughter Mandy is married and lives with her husband Adrian in Sheffield) moved out of the city of Norwich into the countryside in 1993. They moved to a little village called East Lexham in the heart of Norfolk. The village was very peaceful and pretty. This helped inspire Alan to take up watercolour painting once again. In 2004 they moved to another small West Norfolk village near Downham Market where they still live today. In 2008 Alan had to retire due to ill health (bad knees) and whilst he still painted regularly he began to spend more and more time gardening. In 2013 his wife Susie suggested that he kept a gardening diary to record his adventures in the garden and capture the changing seasons, animals, birds and the successes and failures of being a gardener he encountered. By the following year Susie suggested that he should write a book from his diary and include illustrations of both the garden and his artwork. In 2014 Alan's first book was published by Creative Gateway called "Retiring to the Garden – Year One". This proved such a success that Alan decided to follow this up with his second book called "Retiring into a Rainbow" featuring his watercolour paintings. In 2015 Alan published "Retiring to Our Garden – Year Two" published this time by Rainbow Publications UK. He then re-issued his first two books this time in a "Second Edition". Also published by Rainbow Publications UK. In 2016 Alan published: "Skiathos a Greek Island Paradise", "Norfolk the County of my Birth", "Art Inspired by a Rainbow", "Ibiza Island of Dreams", "Majorca Island in the Sun", "Flip-flops and Shades on Thassos", "Mardle and a Troshin' in Norfolk", "England the Country of my Birth", "Mousehole the Cornish Jewel", "Sunshine and Shades on Kefalonia", "Shades and Flip-flops on Zakynthos" and finally "Trips into my Mind's Eye" Also published by Rainbow Publications UK. In 2017, 2018 and 2019 Alan published the following new books entitled: "Corfu and Mainland Greece", "Crete and the Island of Santorini", "Cyprus the Pyramids and the Holy Land", "Greek Islands in the Sun", "Being Greek - The Culture of the People of Greece", "Greece Land of Gods and Men" and finally "Alan's Art Books". In 2020 Alan published new editions of the following books: Trips into my minds eye, Our Garden year 2, Norfolk the country of my Birth, the Paradise Island of Skiathos, Crete and the Island of Santorini, Sunshine and Shades on Kefalonia, Flip-flops and Shades on Thassos and Shades and Flip-flops on Zakynthos also published by Rainbow Publications UK…

Books by Alan R. Massen

Retiring to the Garden Year 1 - Paperback
Retiring into a Rainbow - Paperback and Hardback
Retiring into a Rainbow - 1st Edition - My Favourite Artwork 2020 - 1st Edition
Retiring to our Garden Year one - 1st & 2nd Editions
Retiring to our Garden Year two - 1st & 2nd & 3rd Editions
Retiring into a Rainbow - 1st & 2nd Editions
Skiathos a Greek Island Paradise - 1st & 2nd & 3rd Editions
Norfolk the County of my Birth - 1st & 2nd & 3rd Editions
Art Inspired by a Rainbow - 1st & 2nd & 3rd & 4th Editions
Ibiza Island of Dreams - 1st & 2nd Editions
Majorca Island in the Sun - 1st & 2nd Editions
Flip-Flops and Shades on Thassos - 1st & 2nd & 3rd Editions
Mardle and a Troshin' in Norfolk - 1st & 2nd Editions
England the Country of my Birth - 1st & 2nd Editions
Mousehole the Cornish Jewel - 1st & 2nd & 3rd Editions
Sunshades & Flip-Flops on Kefalonia - 1st & 2nd & 3rd Editions
Shades & Flip-Flops on Zakynthos - 1st & 2nd & 3rd Editions
Trips into my Minds Eye - 1st & 2nd & 3rd & 4th Editions
Corfu and Mainland Greece - 1st & 2nd & 3rd Editions
Crete and the Island of Santorini - 1st & 2nd & 3rd Editions
Cyprus - Pyramids - Holy Land - 1st & 2nd & 3rd Editions
Greek Islands in the Sun - 1st & 2nd & 3rd Editions
Being Greek - 1st & 2nd & 3rd Editions

E-books and Booklets:

Retiring to the Garden Yr 1 - Retiring into a Rainbow - My Art 1997 - 2018 - Skiathos a Greek Paradise Island
My Norfolk - My Greece - My England - My Team - My Skiathos - My Art - My Album of Visual Art
My Village - Greece Land of Gods and Men - Norfolk Wildlife - Civilisation (Empires of the Past)
Boudica Queen of the Iceni - Roman Britain

Alan…

Copyright © 2020 - Alan R. Massen
Published in Great Britain by Rainbow Publications UK.

Books by the same Author

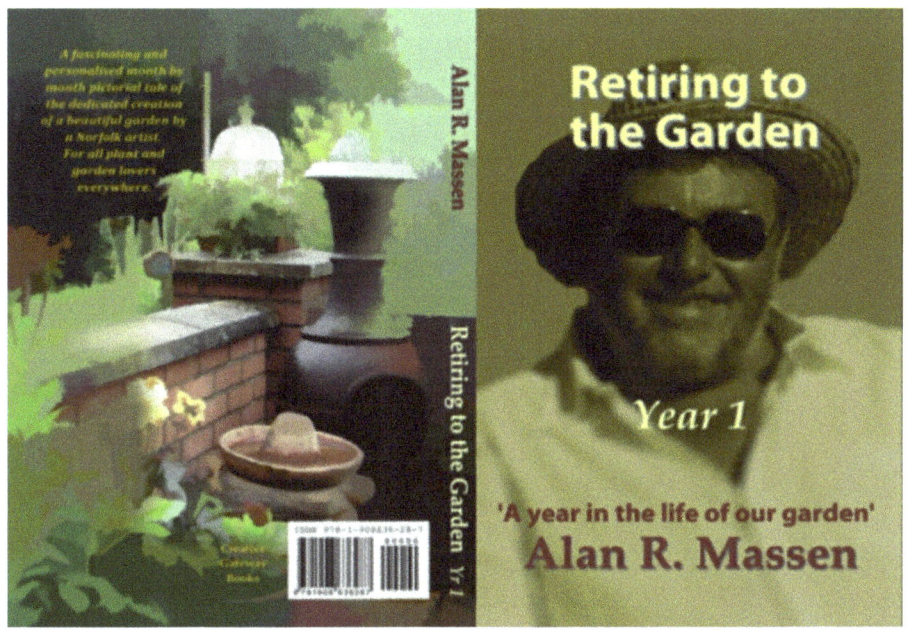

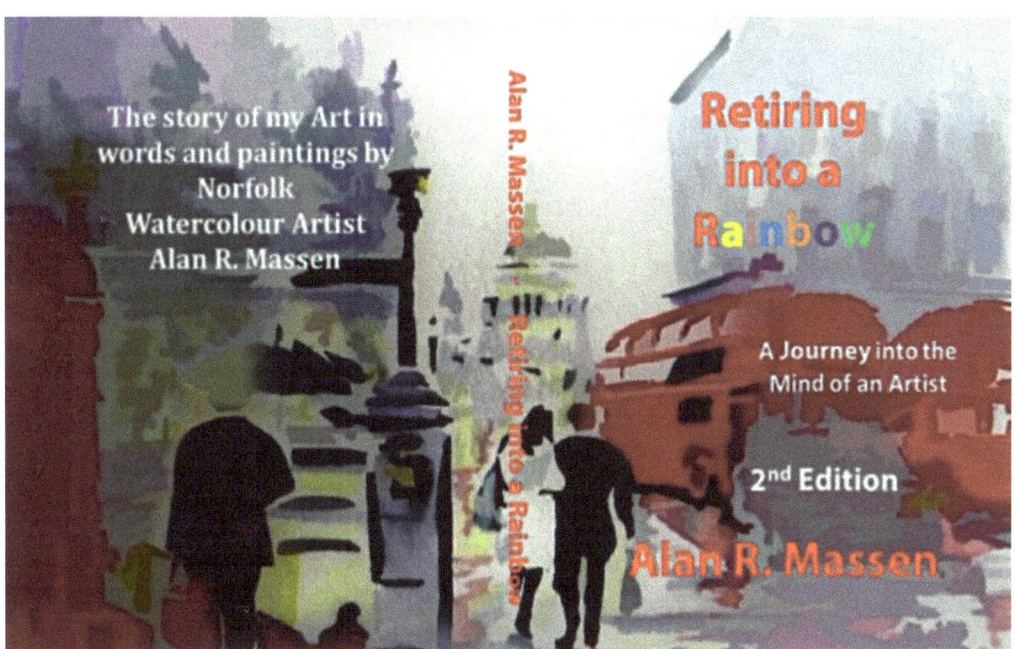

by Norfolk watercolour artist - Alan R. Massen.
Published 1st Editions by Creative Gateway and 2nd Editions by Rainbow Publications UK

Books by the same Author

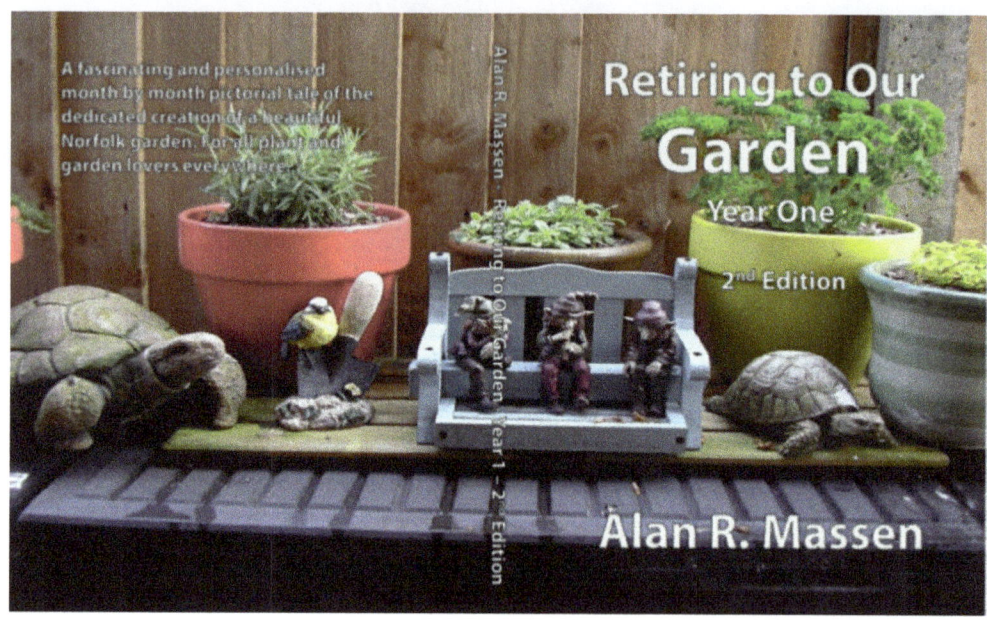

by Norfolk watercolour artist - Alan R. Massen.
Published in Great Britain by Rainbow Publications UK

Books by the same Author

by Norfolk Watercolour Artist - Alan R. Massen
Published in Great Britain by Rainbow Publications UK

Books by the same Author

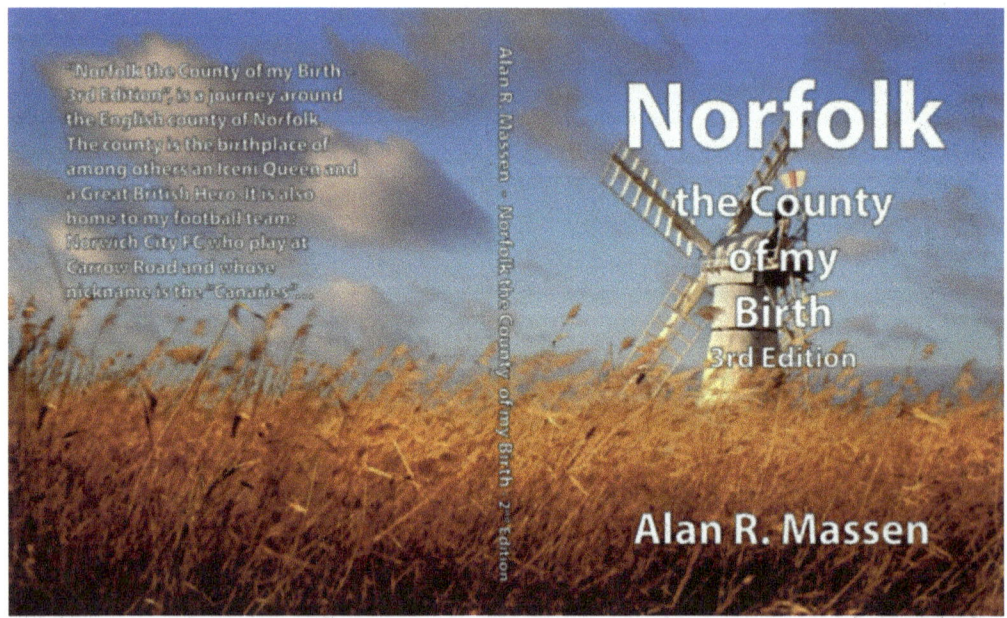

by Norfolk Watercolour Artist - Alan R. Massen
Published in Great Britain by Rainbow Publications UK

Books by the same Author

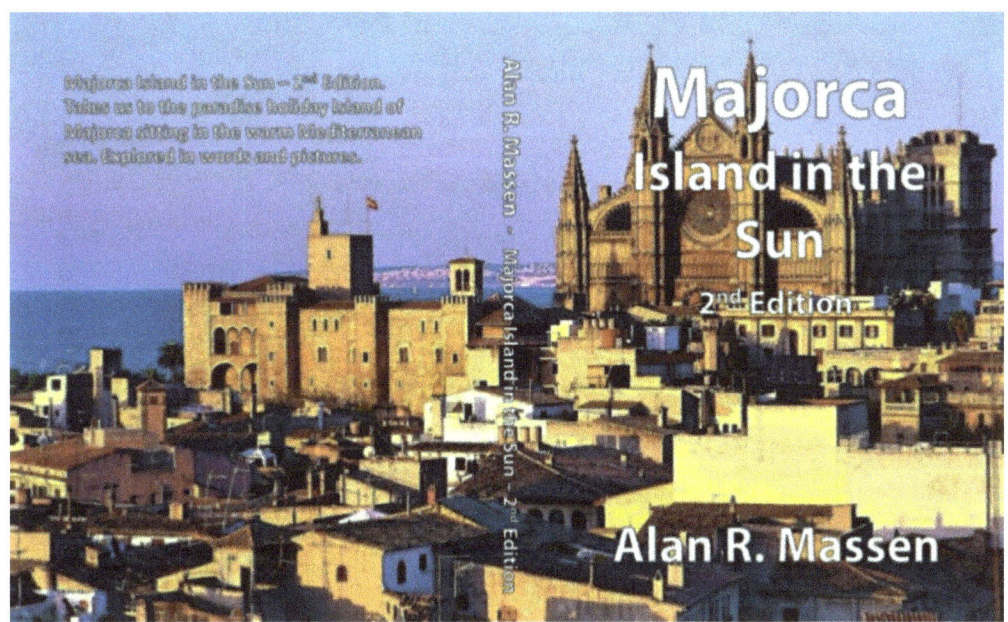

by Norfolk Watercolour Artist - Alan R. Massen
Published in Great Britain by Rainbow Publications UK

Books by the same Author

by Norfolk Watercolour Artist - Alan R. Massen
Published in Great Britain by Rainbow Publications UK

Books by the same Author

by Norfolk Watercolour Artist - Alan R. Massen
Published in Great Britain by Rainbow Publications UK

Books by the same Author

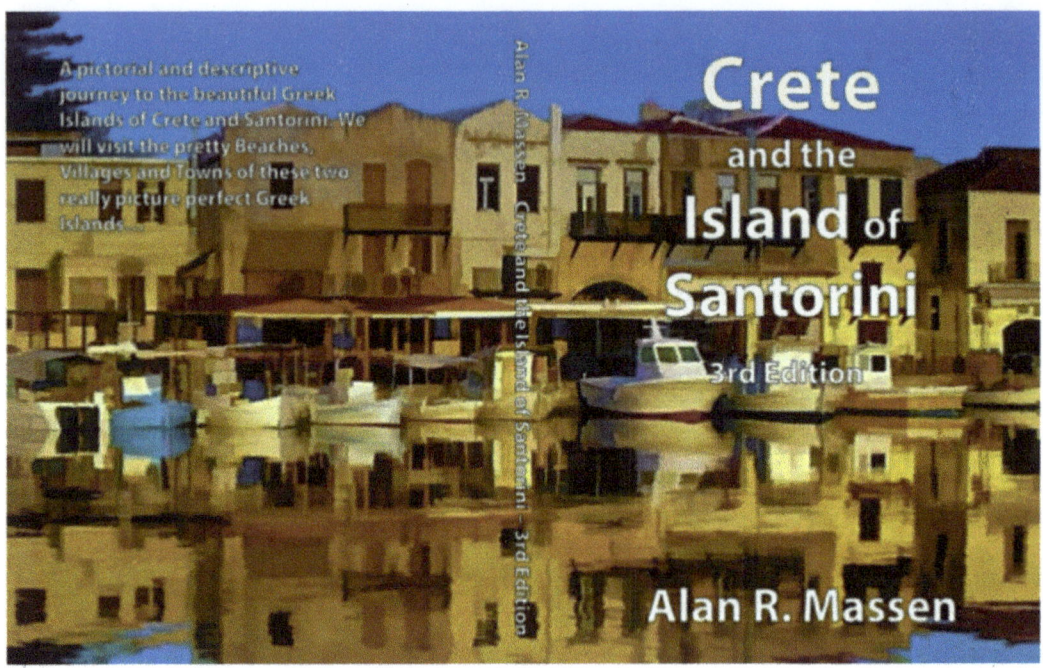

by Norfolk Watercolour Artist - Alan R. Massen
Published in Great Britain by Rainbow Publications UK

Books by the same Author

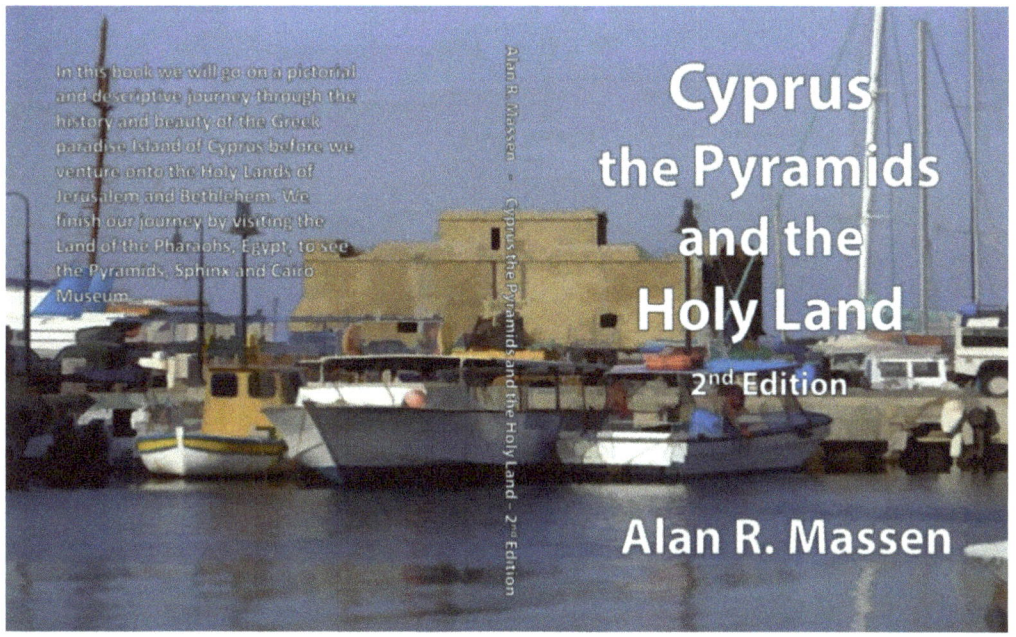

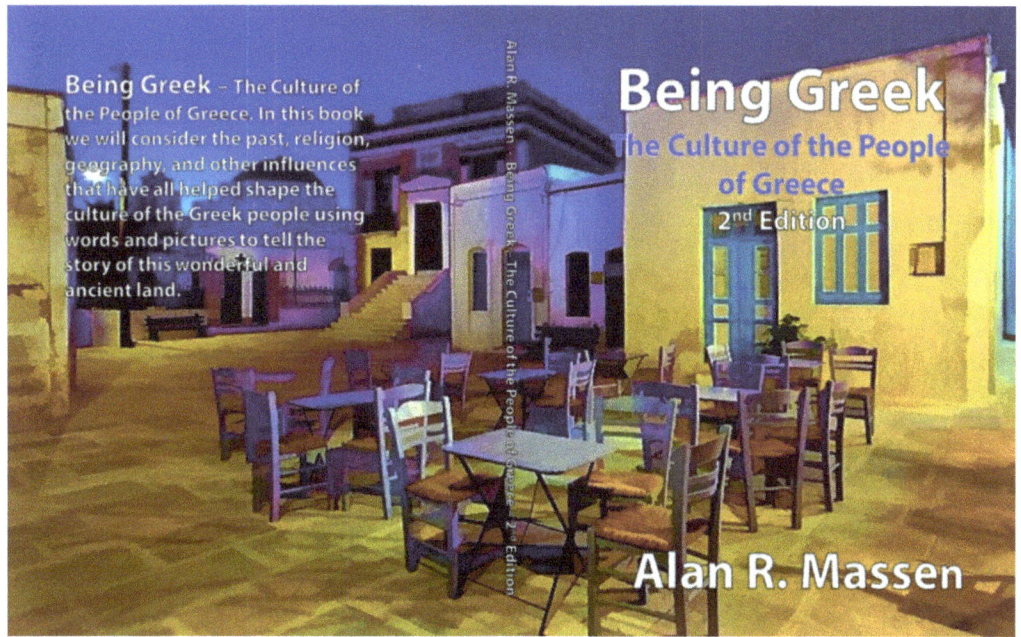

by Norfolk Watercolour Artist - Alan R. Massen
Published in Great Britain by Rainbow Publications UK

Books by the same Author

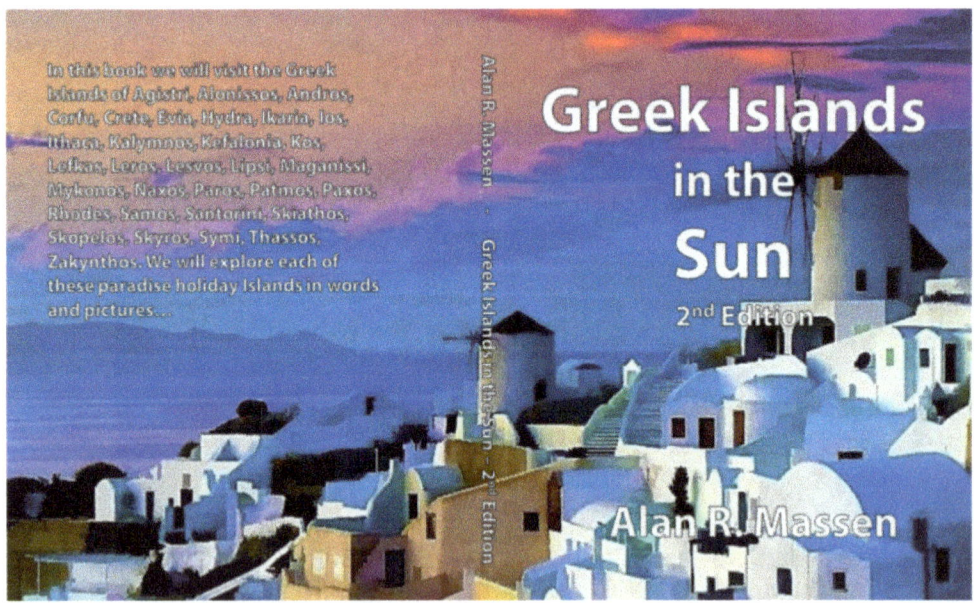

by Norfolk Watercolour Artist - Alan R. Massen
Published in Great Britain by Rainbow Publications UK

Dedication

Welcome to my book called **"Crete and the Island of Santorini"**. I would like to dedicate this book to all those people worldwide who have lost loved ones during the recent terrible Coronavirus pandemic of 2020. All those who have left us will always be remembered and live on in our hearts and minds as we remember all of the love, support and smiles that they shared with us during their lifetimes. I would also like to thank the wonderful, dedicated and brave doctors, nurses and all of the other essential workers who put their own lives at risk to help others during this tragedy. Their bravery has been an inspiration to us all during this awful time and we thank each and to every one of them. **THANK YOU**…

I would also like to dedicate this book to my aunty Joyce, cousin Beryl, daughters Mandy, Ginny, sisters Phyllis, Doreen and my sadly departed Mum, Dad and my son Paul. A special mention to my wife Susie who accompanies me on all of our journeys around the UK and abroad and helps me to enjoy my life to the full every day of my life.

Alan and Susie on holiday…

Latest books by the same Author
Alan's Art Books

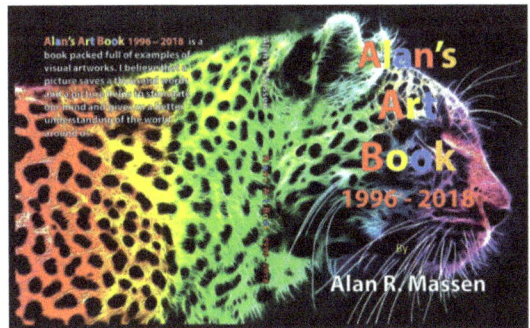
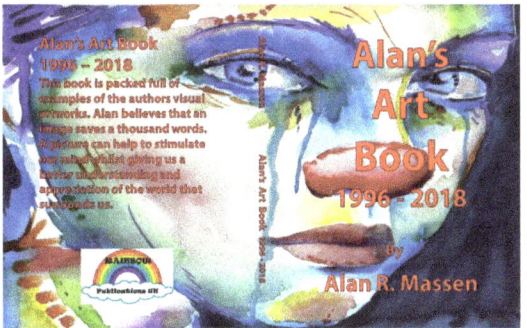

by Norfolk Watercolour Artist Alan R. Massen
Published in Great Britain by Rainbow Publications UK

Contents

Alan and Susie
at the Troulos Bay Hotel
on the Island of Skiathos…

Introduction	1
The History of Crete	19
Facts About Crete	28
Being Greek	53
Out and About on Crete	85
The Best Beaches on Crete	119
Crete in Colour	136
The Island of Santorini	165
Santorini in Colour	192
Acknowledgement	202

Copyright © 2020 Alan R. Massen

Introduction

The Islands of Crete and Santorini are both part of the country of Greece which is located in the south-east of Europe. The islands are located between the Mediterranean and Aegean Seas. The country of Greece includes many Islands, such as Corfu, Thassos, Kos, Ithaca, Rhodes, Crete, Santorini, Kefalonia, Zakynthos, Skiathos, Corfu and many, many more. There is a wealth of accommodation everywhere in Greece to suit all travellers. There are so many ancient and modern places that you can visit on mainland Greece and its Islands. There is something to suit everyone with a wealth of historic sites, sporting venues, walking trails, museums, landmarks, monuments, festivals, carnivals, quality shopping and beautiful cities, towns, villages and wonderful sandy beaches. In this book we will focus on the history, culture and visit many of the great beaches, towns and villages on the lovely Greek Islands of Crete and Santorini…

Introduction

Alan…

In this book you will see numerous examples of my watercolour paintings and/or our photography (holiday snaps taken by Susie and myself) that I have first scanned onto my computer then using a piece of art software, to give these pictures an impressionist style finish, a bit like the artist Claude Monet, to produce the illustrations that I have used extensively throughout this book. I believe, that a picture saves a thousand words and so I hope that you enjoy journeying through this book in words and pictures. Just before we start our exploration of the Islands of Crete and Santorini, I thought, that I ought to introduce myself to you especially for those of you that have not been with me on one of my many other adventures and journeys to places in the UK, the Spanish Islands, the Holy Land, Egypt, mainland Greece and to some of the many paradise Greek Islands that I have written about in my previous books…

Introduction

Alan and St. Nicholas chapel at Georgioupolis on Crete

Hello, my name is Alan and I am married to Susie, we live in a small village in North West Norfolk, England and together, over the last twenty five years, we have been fortunate enough to have had numerous summer holidays both at home and abroad. Our holiday destination of choice, over the years, has usually been to go to one of the many beautiful Greek Islands. We have holidayed on Corfu, Ithaca, Crete, Santorini, Thassos, Kefalonia, Zakynthos and Skiathos to name but a few. We have also during our holidays visited many of the major archaeological sites on the mainland of Greece as well as spending several days visiting the important sites in the City of Athens itself. We have always enjoyed our holidays to the Greek Islands and meeting its warm hearted people. Now you know who I am we will start our journey by first visiting the really beautiful Greek Island of Crete before sailing to visit the Island of Santorini…

Introduction

The Island of Crete

Crete is the largest Island in Greece and the fifth largest Island in the Mediterranean. If you haven't visited the Island of Crete yet, it may now be just the right time to come and discover this fascinating Greek Island for yourself. If you do it may well capture your heart and you will find yourself returning back to its shores year after year…

Introduction

Orange, jasmine blossom and freshly caught octopus on Crete

The Island of Crete

The Island of Crete will always welcome you with its smiling Cretan sun, the sounds of the Cretan lyre, the scents of orange blossom and jasmine, a slice of cool red watermelon and a glass of iced raki. Rakı is an unsweetened, anise-flavored alcoholic drink that is popular in Greece as an apéritif. It is similar to several other alcoholic beverages available around the Mediterranean. It is often served with seafood or a meze (Meze or mezze is a selection of small dishes served to accompany alcoholic drinks as a course or as appetizers before the main dish in Greece). A meze is often served at the beginning of a large-scale meal…

Introduction

The Minoan Palace at Knossos on Crete

The Island of Crete

Crete is an Island with an exquisite 1,000 kilometre-long coastline dotted with numerous coves, bays and peninsulas, which afford a multitude of soft, sandy beaches spread along the beautifully blue Mediterranean Sea. After all, it has beaches that are among the finest in the world. This has helped to establish Crete as one of Europe's most popular holiday destinations. Also Crete has great historical importance and along with the Island of Santorini it is famous as the home of the Minoan civilisation with important archaeological finds found at Knossos, Phaistos and Gortys. These sites are visited by the tens of thousands of visitors every year…

Introduction

The Island of Santorini

Santorini, classically known as Thera, and officially Thira, is an Island in the southern Aegean Sea, about 200 km southeast of the Greek mainland…

Introduction

The Island of Santorini

Santorini is the largest Island of a small, circular archipelago which bears the same name and is the remnant of a volcanic caldera. A volcanic caldera is a large cauldron-like volcanic depression, a type of volcanic crater, formed by the collapse of an emptied magma chamber. The depression often originates in very big explosive eruptions. The emptying of this magma chamber may also be accomplished more gradually by a series of effusive eruptions from the volcanic system which can be kilometers away from the magma chamber itself…

Introduction

Ancient remains on the island of Delos

The Island of Santorini

The Island of Santorini forms the southernmost member of the Cyclades group of Islands. The Cyclades are a group of Islands in the south Aegean Sea. They get their name from the Greek word 'Kyklos' which means circle as all the Islands seem to circle the sacred ancient Island of Delos almost like a wheel on an axis…

Introduction

The Island of Santorini

Out of the many Islands that make up Greece the Cyclades are easily the most popular and most visited. There are actually 54 Islands in the Cyclades group but only 24 of these are inhabited. Santorini has an area of approximately 73 km² and in a 2011 census it had a local population of 15,550. The municipality of Santorini includes the inhabited Islands of Santorini and Therasia and the uninhabited Islands of Nea Kameni, Palaia Kameni, Aspronisi, and Christiana. Its total land area is 90.623 km². Santorini is part of the Thira regional unit…

Introduction

Minoan Wall Art…

Knossos a Minoan palace on Crete

The Minoan civilisation

The Minoan civilisation was an Aegean Bronze Age civilisation that arose on the Islands of Crete, Santorini and other Aegean Islands and flourished from approximately 3650 to 1400 BC. The myth of the Minotaur and the Labyrinth has preserved the memory of the unique Minoan civilisation from antiquity right through the ages up to the present day. It was a civilisation where the bull was worshipped and majestic structures like that at Knossos Palace on Crete existed in all of their Minoan glory…

Introduction

The remains of the Minoan town of Akrotiri on Santorini…

The Minoan civilisation

The bull-man Minotaur was depicted in religious ceremonies of the time where the priests wore masks in the shape of a bull's head. In the ancient Greek language, the word Labyrinth means "the house of lavrys." The lavrys is the double-edged axe and is one of the basic sacred symbols of the Minoan religion. Usually interpreted as a solar symbol, the lavrys is etched on many sculptured stones in Minoan palaces and other buildings, as well as on vases, pots, and various other works of art. The Minotaur, man or beast, lives or hides in the Labyrinth. Initially, the Labyrinth was associated with the palace at Knossos on the Island of Crete…

Introduction

The killing of the Minotaur

The Minoan civilisation

Myth says that Icarus and his father Daedalus were imprisoned in the Labyrinth by King Minos, as punishment for the help Daedalus gave Queen Pasiphae and Ariadne, daughter of King Minos. The cunning Daedalus, however, found a way to escape: he made two pairs of wings from feathers and wax, one for himself and one for Icarus. They used these to fly from their prison, the first recorded flight in history, two thousand years before the Wright Brothers. The Minoan civilisation belongs to a period of Greek history preceding both the Mycenaean and Ancient Greek civilisations…

Introduction

Mycenaean gold death mask and a citadel grave circle

The Mycenaean Age

The Mycenaean Age dates from around 1600 BC to 1100 BC, during the Bronze Age. Mycenae is an archaeological site in Greece from which the name Mycenaean Age is derived. Mycenae sites are located on the mainland in the Peloponnese region of southern Greece…

Introduction

Mycenaean lions gate and gold cup

The Mycenaean Age

Prior to the Mycenaean's ascendancy in Greece, the Minoan culture was dominant. However, the Mycenaeans defeated the Minoans, acquiring the famous city of Troy in the process. The Mycenaeans also inhabited the ruins of Knossos on Crete, which was a major city during the Minoan era. Mycenaean and Minoan art merged, forming a cultural amalgamation that is found on the Island of Crete today (figurines, sculptures and pottery). The Mycenaeans invented their own script known as Linear B, which was an improved derivative of Linear A. This is the language which is commonly accepted as being that of the ancient Minoan…

Introduction

The Ancient Greek Civilisation

The Ancient Greek civilisation belonged to a period of Greek history that lasted from the archaic period of the 8th to 6th centuries BC to the end of antiquity. Immediately following this period was the beginning of the Roman era which was from 69 AD until 330 AD the Early Middle Ages and the Byzantine era. Included in the ancient Greek era is the period known as the Classical Greek period, which flourished during the 5th to 4th centuries BC…

Introduction

Persians attacking Athens and Alexander the Great

The Classical Greek Period

The Classical Greece era began with the repelling of a Persian invasion by the Athenians. Because of the conquests by Alexander the Great of Macedonia, Hellenistic civilisation flourished from Central Asia to the western end of the Mediterranean Sea during this period…

Introduction

The Minoans on Santorini

Summary

The Minoan civilisation was rediscovered at the beginning of the 20th century through the work of British archaeologist Arthur Evans. Historian Will Durant dubbed the Minoans "the first link in the European chain," and their civilisation has been referred to as the earliest of its kind in Europe. So now that we know where the Islands of Crete and Santorini are and learnt about the rich historical thread that links these two Greek Island we will start our journey together. In the next chapter we will be concentrating on the wider history of Greece before focusing on discovering the history, culture, beaches, towns, villages and countryside of the Island of Crete. Once we have explored Crete we will continue our voyage of discovery by visiting the beautiful Island of Santorini…

The History of Crete

Greece Land of Gods and Men

The position of Greece at the crossroads between Africa, Asia, and Europe has undeniably played an important role in the diverse and often turbulent history of Greece. Protruding from Europe, Greece hangs precariously south from the end of the Balkan Peninsula, and slices into the Mediterranean Sea . Greece has dramatic peninsulas and thousands of large and small Islands. The Mediterranean Sea has a climate of generally mild winters and hot, dry summers, while its mountainous terrain, allowed for multiple easily defensible positions. The surrounding sea offered an environment conducive to developing and sustaining an enduring culture that was relatively safe from incursions while able to communicate and exchange large quantities of goods and ideas with ease through the sea lanes. It is therefore, not by accident that the ancient Greek civilisation developed around a significant maritime power…

The History of Crete

Ancient Greece

Today the country of Greece is contained within its modern borders, in the ancient Hellenic civilisation times it expanded its influence throughout the Mediterranean. As well as the traditional Greek mainland, its Islands, and the coastal margins of Asia Minor, Hellenic colonies existed in Italy, Sicily, France, Spain, Libya, and all around the Black Sea. Following the conquests of Alexander the Great Hellenic civilisation attained its widest reach. During the Hellenistic era Greek culture expanded to include Asia Minor, the Middle East, Egypt, and the land further East to the Western parts of India, and as far north as today's country of Afghanistan some experts even suggest that their influence reached as far as China…

The History of Crete

Queen Europa of the Island of Crete and island map

Crete Mythology and Legends

The Crete history is long and marked by many historical periods. According to Greek mythology, the first queen of Crete was Europa. later on, Crete Island became the land of King Minos. The legend is that the King refused to sacrifice a bull to the gods and Poseidon punished him by making his wife fall in love with a bull. From this union the Minotaur was born and was hid in a labyrinth at Knossos Palace on Crete. Another legend says that to avenge the death of his son by the Athenians, King Minos made them send seven young girls and boys to Crete every year, to offer them as a sacrifice to the Minotaur. During an expedition the famous mythical hero Theseus, the son of the King of Athens, left Athens with the young Athenians and, with the help of Ariadne, the daughter of King Minos, managed to kill the Minotaur and find his way out of the labyrinth. It is said that he unwound a line of string as he entered the labyrinth and then used this to find his way back out again after killing the beast…

The History of Crete

Minoan Palace at Knossos and the Minoan Palace at Phaestos

Crete in Ancient Times

Ancient Crete is the place where, it is believed, the Minoan civilisation, one of the most important civilisations of the world (2600-1150 BC), started. Huge palace-states were built, such as the famous and superb palaces of Knossos Palace, Phaestos Palace and Zakros Palace. The Minoans also established a strong naval empire in the Mediterranean…

The History of Crete

The Archaeological Site at Akrotiri on the Island of Santorini

Crete in Ancient Times

The Minoan civilisation was ended by a natural disaster: the huge waves caused by the eruption of the volcano on the Island of Santorini in 1450 BC. The eruption and subsequent huge wave covered the northern coasts of Crete with high waves, lava ash and sand. This disaster was followed by the invasion of the Achaeans and the Dorians, tribes from Northern Europe which meant that the Minoan civilisation was never able to be revived. The architecture of the ancient sites and temples proves the great wealth of the culture that was on the Island since antiquity…

The History of Crete

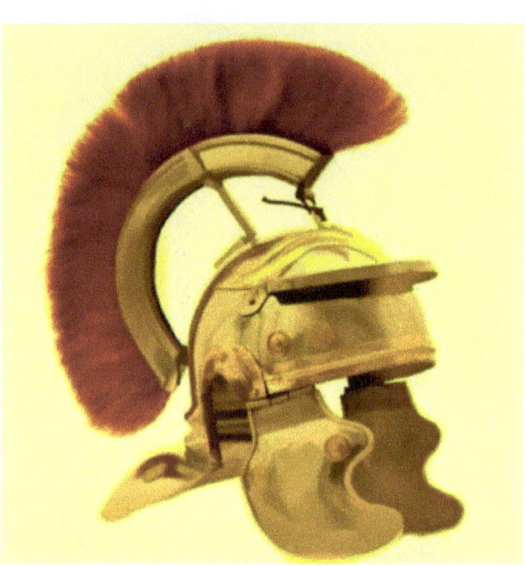

Crete in Roman and Byzantine times

The Roman occupation of Crete came in 69 AD and lasted until 330 AD. It was followed by the Byzantine era during which the wealth of Crete was still visible in the beautiful mosaic floors of the basilicas that were built during that period…

The History of Crete

The Cities of Venice, Heraklion and some Ottoman Turk fighters

The Venetian and Ottoman Occupation

The Island of Crete fell under the domination of the Arabs, in 824 AD, and stayed under it for 137 years. During those years the city of Heraklion was founded. It was first called by the name of Handak. During the early Byzantine years, several churches and structures were constructed. In 1204, the Venetians founded new fortified cities after they had conquered the Island of Crete. They also fortified the old castles built by the Arabs and even built new castles…

The History of Crete

The Venetian and Ottoman occupation of Crete

The old towns of Rethymno (see above - top) and Chania (see above - bottom) have remained intact since the Renaissance, with their beautifully decorated squares, superb fountains and fine churches and palaces. During those years, the arts flourished such as painting and literature. In this period many artists and scholars from Constantinople came to the Island of Crete. In 1669, the Island fell under Ottoman rule which lasted until 1897, when the great statesman of Greece, Eleftherios Venizelos, negotiated the independence of the Island of Crete. Crete was declared an autonomous state and, in 1913 it was united with the independent Greek State…

The History of Crete

The Island of Crete in the 20th Century

During World War II, Crete played a major role in the war. The stiff resistance that the Germans encountered on the Island caught them completely off guard. Eventually, all of Crete fell under German occupation. Many of the local residents were executed for their participation in the Resistance War against the German invasion and many villagers were massacred. As the war continued Islanders escaped from the south of Crete on ships that would secretly come in at night to board people to escape to Egypt, so that they could continue their war against the Germans from there. Today Crete is a large Island that gets most of its income from agriculture, cattle breeding and tourism. Although there are tourist places all over the Island, the inhabitants still keep their old traditions and customs alive. In fact, tradition is very important to them even in their everyday life…

Facts about Crete

The Island of Crete

Crete's largest modern town is called Heraklion (see above) and its landscape oscillates between tall, rugged mountains, gentle slopes and plateaus, which are framed by the Aegean Sea to the North, and the Libyan Sea to the south…

Facts about Crete

The Climate of Crete

The climate of Crete with its short, mild winters and its dry, warm summers, along with the fertility of the Cretan plains all contribute in the production of sufficient food to support the Islands population, and even some for export. In ancient times the inhabitants of the Island of Crete who were called the Minoans, had a decentralised culture that was based on the abundance of the land's natural resources, and on intense commercial seafaring activity…

Facts about Crete

Crete the land of honey and wine

The Island of Crete today appears completely deforested, in ancient times timber was one of the abundant natural resources that was commercially exploited and exported to nearby Egypt, Syria, Cyprus, the Aegean Islands and the Greek mainland. As well as timber the Island of Crete exported cypress wood, good quality wine, currants, olive oil, wool, cloth, herbs, honey and purple dye. Its imports consisted of precious stones, copper (most likely from the Island of Cyprus), ivory, silver, gold, and other raw material. They also imported tin that was used in the production of bronze alloys. Interestingly, the nearest known tin mines are located as far away as Spain, Britain, central Europe, and Iran. Besides raw materials, the Minoans also adopted, from the surrounding cultures, artistic ideas and techniques as evident in Egypt's influence on the Minoan wall frescoes, and on gold production knowledge that was imported from Syria…

Facts about Crete

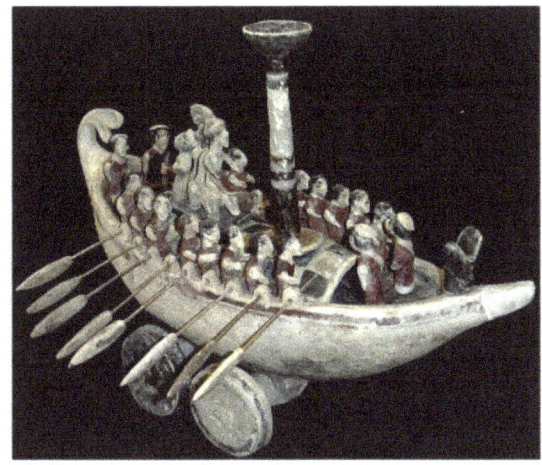

Ancient Minoan ship and wall fresco of bull leaping

The Cretan Minoans

The Minoans had developed significant naval power and for many centuries they were in contact with all the major civilisations of the time without being significantly threatened by external forces. Their commercial contact with ancient Egypt and Mesopotamia undeniably influenced their own culture, and the Minoan civilisation in turn appeared as the forerunner of the Greek civilisation. The Minoans on the Island of Crete and the Island of Santorini are credited as being the very first European civilisation…

Facts about Crete

The Minoan Palace at Knossos

The Cretan Minoans

Archaeological evidence testifies to the Island's habitation since the 7th millennium BC After the 5th millennium BC we find the first evidence of hand-made ceramic pottery which marks the beginning of the civilisation. Evans, the famed archaeologist who excavated Knossos, named "Minoan" after the legendary King Minos. Evans divided the Minoan civilisation into three eras on the basis of the stylistic changes of the pottery. His comparative chronology included an Early (3000-2100 BC), a Middle (2100-1500 BC), and a Late Minoan period (1500-1100 BC). There is little known information about the very early Minoans before 2600 BC. At first there had been the development of several minor settlements near the coast, and the beginning of burials in Tholos tombs, as well as in caves around the Island during this early period…

Facts about Crete

Early Minoan Crete (2600-1900 BC)

Neolithic life in ancient Crete consisted of major settlements at Myrtos and Mochlos. During this period the Minoans had contact with Egypt, Asia Minor, and Syria with whom they traded for copper, tin, ivory, and gold. The archaeological evidence reveals a decentralised culture with no powerful landlords and no centralised authority…

Facts about Crete

Early Minoan Crete (2600-1900 BC)

The palaces of this period were focused around communities, and circular tholos tombs were the major architectural structures of the time. The manner by which the dead were buried in these tombs indicate a society without hierarchical structure. The tholos tombs were used for centuries by entire villages, or clans and older corpses and offerings were moved to one side to make room for a new burial. Older bones were then removed from the tomb and placed in bone chambers outside the tholos structure. A practice that is still used in Greece today. Most of the tholos tombs were circular while in Palekastro and Mochlos they were rectangular in shape with a flat roof…

Facts about Crete

Middle Minoan Crete (1900-1700 BC)

The middle Minoan era began with social upheaval, external dangers, and migrations from mainland Greece and Asia Minor. During this time the Minoans began establishing colonies on Thera, Rodos, Melos, and Kithira. Around 2000 BC a new political system was established with authority concentrated around a central figure of the King. The first large palaces were built and acted as centres for their respective communities, while at the same time they developed a bureaucratic administration which permeated right through Minoan society. Distinctions between the classes forged a social hierarchy and divided the people into nobles, peasants, and perhaps even slaves…

Facts about Crete

Middle Minoan Crete (1900-1700 BC)

In the Middle Minoan period after its tumultuous beginning, was a peaceful and prosperous period for the Minoans who continued to trade with Egypt and the Middle East, while they constructed a paved road network to connect their major cultural centres on the Island…

Facts about Crete

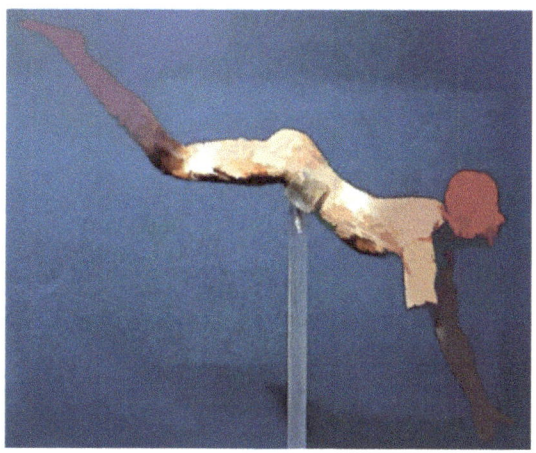

Minoan bull jumping figurine and dolphin fresco

Middle Minoan Crete (1900-1700 BC)

In the Middle Minoan period saw the development of some settlements outside the palaces, and the end of the extensive use of tholos tombs. The palaces of the period were then destroyed in 1700 BC by forces that remain unknown. Speculation blames the destruction either on a powerful earthquake, or on outside invaders. Despite the abrupt destruction of the palaces however, Minoan civilisation continued to flourish on the Islands of Crete and Santorini…

Facts about Crete

Late Minoan Crete (1700-1400 BC)

In the late Minoan era the destroyed palaces were rebuilt on the ruins of the old palaces to form even more spectacular structures. This is the time when Knossos, Phaistos, Malia, and Zakros were built together with many smaller palaces which stretched along the Cretan landscape. Small towns developed near the palaces. For the first time smaller residencies that today we would call villas appeared in the rural landscape, and were modelled after the large palaces with storage facilities, workshops and places for worshipping the Gods…

Facts about Crete

Late Minoan Crete (1700-1400 BC)

During the late Minoan period there is evidence of administrative and economic unity throughout the Island, and Minoan Crete reach its zenith. Women played a powerful role in society, and the gold artifacts, seals, and spears speak of a very affluent upper class. The paved road network was vastly expanded to connect most major Minoan palaces and towns, and there was extensive trade activity. The Minoan culture's fusion with the Helladic (mainland Greek) traditions of the time eventually morphed into the Mycenaean civilisation, which in turn challenged the sea supremacy of the Minoans in the Aegean…

Facts about Crete

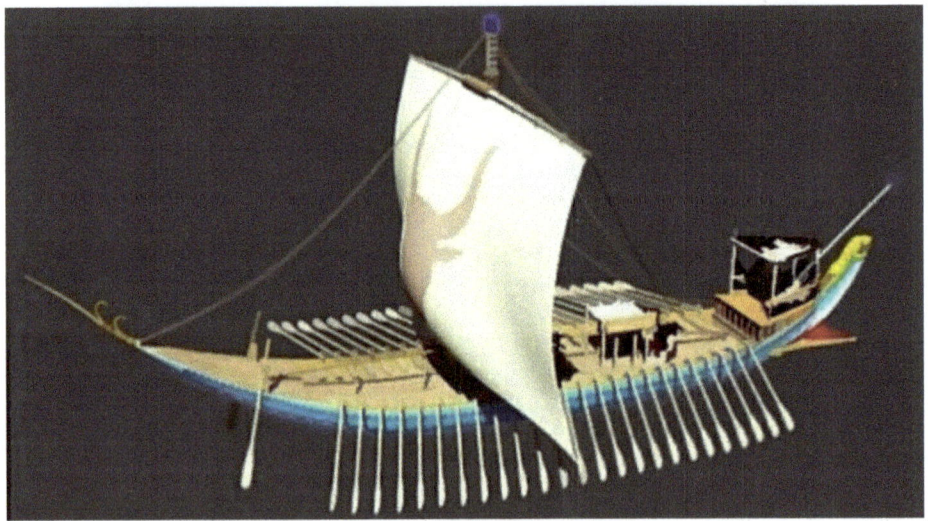

The End of Minoan Crete

For the first time, late in the Minoan period, the powerful fleet of the Minoans encountered competition from an emerging power from mainland Greece: the Mycenaeans whose influence began permeating Minoan Crete itself. Life on the Island became more militaristic as evident by the large number of weapons and fine pottery which have been found for the first time in royal tombs. The affluence of the culture during this period is evident in the frescoes found in the Cretan palaces and in the palaces on the Islands of Thera (Santorini), Melos, Kea, and Rodos…

Facts about Crete

The End of Minoan Crete

The end of this flourishing culture came with the destruction of most of the palaces and villas in the country side in the middle of the 15 century, and with the destruction of Knossos in 1375 BC. During this late period there is evidence in tablets inscribed in Linear B language that the Mycenaeans controlled the entire Island, while many Minoan sites had been abandoned for a long time. It is impossible to be certain of the causes for this sudden interruption of the Minoan civilisation. However scholars have pointed to invasion of outside forces, or to the colossal eruption of the Thera volcano on the Island of Santorini as likely causes…

Facts about Crete

The weather of Crete

The weather of Crete is characterised by mild, rainy winters and hot, dry summers. So the climate of Crete is a temperate Mediterranean climate. There are significant differences between the coastal zone and the mountainous areas, as well as between the west and the eastern part of Crete, when it comes to the weather conditions. The mountains of Crete form an East-West barrier to prevailing northerly winds and they trap the clouds sweeping down the Aegean Sea. The result is that it may be grey and wet in the north, but sunny on the south coast where often the clouds do not extend out over the sea…

Facts about Crete

The weather of Crete

As we have already seen the weather in the coastal areas of Crete is dry in the summer and mild in the winter. The rainy season on the Island starts in late October and lasts until March or even into April. Snowfalls are extremely rare in the coastal zone of Crete, especially so in the eastern part of the Island. The eastern part of Crete (Sitia area) is drier and warmer than the western part (Chania district). This is obvious in the vegetation of the area. Chania is a lot greener than the desert-like Sitia area. The same difference applies between the north coast and the south coast of Crete, with the south coast being drier and warmer…

Facts about Crete

The weather of Crete

The winter in the mountainous area of Crete can be very cold with significant amounts of snowfall. It is not unusual for the roads of the Island to be closed due to heavy snowfalls. Up in the high summits of Mt Ida and the White Mountains (see above) the snow stays on the mountain sides until late June…

Facts about Crete

Summary of the weather of Crete

January: Cold, rainy and windy. There is a one-week period during January when the weather is generally good and the winds cease. This period is called the Halcyon Days.

February: Slightly warmer and sunnier than January. The almond trees bloom in February, the first trees to bloom on the Island. The weather is unpredictable and cold days alternate with warm ones.

March: Usually cold and windy but there are many sunny days too. In March 2001 there was a heat wave with temperatures as high as 30 °C but that was an exception. The first daring swimmers appeared in the sea.

April: Spring time in Crete with medium temperatures and low rainfall. Crete is full of wildflowers and it is magnificent to visit at this time of the year.

May: The weather in Crete becomes warm and sunny. Rain is unlikely to occur past May 10th. The "meltemi" seasonal North winds have not yet started to blow, the sea is calm and nature is at its best. May is considered the best month for outdoor activities. A jacket will prove useful at night.

June: Sunny and hot makes it the ideal time for the beach…

Facts about Crete

Summary of the weather of Crete

July and August: Windy and very hot. July and August are the months that the seasonal North winds blow. It is hard to do anything else during these months, than spend the entire day at the beach. Look for a shady place and drink plenty of water. Do not forget your hat and sunscreen. Not the best weather for people who cannot stand high temperatures (30-35 C).

September: Sunny, less windy and slightly cooler. Good for outdoors activities. Get a light jacket for the night, especially if you plan to visit any mountainous areas.

October: Sunny, very few windy days but some rain will fall, especially in the west part of Crete. The weather is very good for outdoor activities. October is the month that the traditional drink of Crete, raki, is distilled from grape skins. Warm clothes are rarely necessary.

November: The weather becomes unpredictable. It may be sunny but there are plenty of rainy and windy days too. Pack a sweater and don't forget your umbrella. The south winds start and sometimes they carry sand from the Sahara desert in Africa. This sand covers the sky of Crete and it creates very unusual weather conditions.

December: The weather conditions vary from year to year with a mixture of windy, calm, rainy, sunny, cold and warm days. Pack warm clothes together with your swimming suit. There are days when the temperature along the south coast makes swimming possible and can be very pleasurable…

Facts about Crete

The food of Crete

Susie and I love Greek food. It is always fresh and delicious. Olive oil plays a central role in Greek food preparation and is used also to accompany most meals. When we are on holiday in Greece Susie and I enjoy nothing better than sitting in a seafront taverna and enjoying the great views and wonderful food with plenty of local wine and mythos beer while people watching. When we are back at home Susie often cooks us traditional Greek food for our main meals or to have as snacks outside. You just cannot beat feta and olives with a glass of wine. In the next few pages I will share with you some of the recipes Susie uses when she cooks Greek! I hope that you will try these for yourself or order them when you next visit Greece…

Facts about Crete

The food of Crete

All the recipes that follow are Traditional Recipes from Crete.

Olive Pate: Place in a bowl 250 g of black olives without their stones, 80 g of anchovies washed and thinly cut, 50 g of caper and mush these all together. Add the juice of one lemon, a tablespoon of brandy, 200 g olive oil, salt, pepper and stir well. Keep the pate in a closed jar in the fridge and use on bread preferably that has been lightly toasted.

Baked Fish: Wash, salt and bake on the grill 4-5 fish slices - preferably sea bream or grouper. In a bowl, mix two medium, ripe tomatoes thinly sliced, a cup of extra virgin olive oil, a tablespoon of thinly cut parsley, juice of half a lemon, salt and pepper. Serve the fish while still hot, after you have first covered it with the tomato and olive oil sauce…

Facts about Crete

The food of Crete

Chicken with Olives: Cut a chicken in small portions and lay it in a pot in which you have already poured a teacup of olive oil. Cut 2 green peppers, 2 red peppers, 2 onions and two garlic cloves into thin pieces. De-pip 12 olives and together with two ripe tomatoes thinly cut and a large cup of red wine add all of these ingredients to the chicken and bake in an oven for about 1 1/2 hours, until all of the liquid has been absorbed then serve.

Granny's Fried Potatoes: Peel and cut two large potatoes into thick wedge shaped pieces and place in a pot, salt them, sprinkle them with the juice of half a lemon and stir them well. Cover and leave for about 45 minutes. In a deep frying pan, heat up 2 cups of virgin olive oil. Drop the potatoes in the hot olive oil and let them fry with no cover until they get golden. Take them out with a strainer-ladle and place them onto kitchen paper towels so that they totally drain from any excess oil. They are traditionally eaten hot…

Facts about Crete

The food of Crete

Fried Olives: How to prepare: into a bowl put an egg, salt, pepper, a little dusting of flour and mix. Always use black olives. Take out the olive stones and stir them into the mix in the bowl that you prepared earlier. With a spoon, take the coated olives out of the mixture and fry in hot olive oil.

Eggs and Tomato: Put in a frying pan a couple of big, ripe tomatoes, skinned and thinly sliced, salt them and simmer them for about 6-7 minutes, until they absorb all the liquid. Add 6 tablespoons of extra virgin olive oil and stir for 2-3 minutes. Add 4 eggs, sprinkle with pepper and fry on low heat for a few more minutes, occasionally stirring the sauce around. If you wish, you can add a bit of grated feta cheese. Serve the eggs and tomato with the sauce and olive oil…

Facts about Crete

The food of Crete

Yoghurt Pie with Olive Oil: In a bowl, whisk together a cup of olive oil and two cups of sugar. Add gradually the yolks of 6 eggs, the shavings off the skin of a lemon, a small-medium bowl of Greek yoghurt, 3 teacups of flour (in which you have added 3 teaspoons of baking powder) and the whites of the eggs that you have previously whisked into meringue. Place the mixture on a baking tray and bake in a medium oven.

Olive-Bread with Rosemary: In a bowl, stir 1 kg of flour with 2 spoonful's of dry yeast and a spoonful of oregano. Add a spoonful of sugar, 2 teaspoons of salt, 80 g of olive oil, 2 cups of warm water and knead until the dough goes soft. Leave the dough covered in a warm place until it puffs up. When it does, lay it and spread it on an oiled baking tray, pressing it lightly so that it is flat and even, oil it and make little cavities by pressing the dough with your fingers, where you then place 150 g of Kalamata olives (without their stone) and the leaves of rosemary. Bake in a medium oven for about an hour. Serve hot.

Cauliflower Casserole with Tomatoes and Spices: Clean and cut a large cauliflower into pieces, sprinkled it with the juice of 1-2 lemons and add salt and pepper. Brown the pieces in a frying pan with heated olive oil and place them one by one into a boiling pot. When they are finished, slowly brown in the same oil add a medium onion thinly cut and add a tablespoon of tomato puree thinned in water. After it has gone through a couple of boils, empty the frying pan contents into the boiling pot, add a glass of water and let it simmer until all liquids but the oil have been absorbed…

Facts about Crete

The food of Crete

Pork with Spinach: Brown 4 portions of pork meat in virgin olive oil. In a bowl, thin a tablespoon of tomato puree in 2 glasses of water and add the thinly cut skin of an orange, salt, pepper, and use all of this mixture to sprinkle over the meat. Wash 1 kg of spinach and a bunch of celery. When the meat is half done, add the greens and cook until the greens are cooked.

Tabulee: In a bowl, put 100 g of crushed grain in a little cold water so that it puffs up. Wash 2 bunches of parsley, a bunch of mint and fresh onions, drain them and slice them. Drain the crushed grain by hand, put it in a salad bowl and add salt, pepper, the juice of half a lemon and virgin olive oil, stirring slowly. Add the cut greens, the rest of the lemon juice and a large tomato, cut into pieces. Serve with bread and freshly washed lettuce leaves.

After enjoying all of this lovely food it is now time to get up from our table and make our way into the next chapter were we will discover what **being Greek** is all about…

Being Greek

Almost since time began Greece has been recognised as the birthplace of civilisation and democracy. Athens is one of the oldest cities in Europe. Greece and Athens in particular is also seen as the birthplace of democracy, Western philosophy, the Olympic Games, political science, Western literature, historiography, major mathematical principles, and Western theories of tragedy and comedy. Greece has given man its Gods of Mythology, the Olympic Games, The Parthenon, Minoan Culture and much, much more. In more recent times it has been the country of choice for a vast number of visitors (tourists) both to see its ancient cultural heritage sites, cities and/or to visit its multitude of paradise Islands. Greece has an abundance of fabulous beaches, rugged scenery and a warm, welcoming and friendly people…

Being Greek

Being Greek

Susie and I have spent many a happy summer holiday on one of the many Greek Islands as well as being lucky enough to be able to visit many of the important ancient sites and cities on the mainland over the last twenty five years. During our holidays in Greece we have met and befriended many of the local population. We have, over the years, been told by our Greek hosts many interesting facts about Greece, its customs and its people. We have found these facts very interesting and enlightening. They explain many things about the Greeks and their ways that we did not understand and so I have included these facts in the pages that follow so you too can begin to understand what it is "**Being Greek**"…

Being Greek

Greece has an area of 50,949 square miles (131,958 square kilometres), Greece is roughly the size of Alabama. The population of Greece is more than 10 million people.

Greece attracts approximately 16.5 million tourists that visit Greece each year which is more than the country's entire population. Tourism constitutes nearly 16% of the Gross Domestic Product (GDP) of Greece.

In Greece everyone has to vote. Voting is required by law for every citizen who is 18 or older.

Greece produces about 7% of all of the marble produced in the world comes from Greece.

Greece has more international airports than most other countries in the world because there are so many foreign tourists that want to visit its shores.

Greece is the world's third leading producer of olives, the Greeks have cultivated olive trees since ancient times. Some olive trees planted in the thirteenth century are still producing olives today…

Being Greek

According to Greek mythology, Athena and Poseidon agreed that whoever gave the city of Athens the best gift would become guardian over the city. Though Poseidon gave the gift of water, Athena's gift of an olive tree was deemed by the other gods to be more valuable and so she became guardian of the city of Athens.

It is a fact that Greece has zero navigable rivers this is because of the mountainous terrain. Nearly 80% of Greece is mountainous.

In Greece approximately 98% of the people are ethnic Greeks. Turks form the largest minority group. Other minorities are Albanians, Macedonians, Bulgarians, Armenians, and gypsies.

About 12 million people around the world speak Greek. They live mostly in Greece, Cyprus, Italy, Albania, Turkey and the United States of America, among other countries.

Thousands of English words come from the Greek language, sometimes via the Roman adaptation into Latin and then into English. Common English words from Greek include "academy," "apology," "marathon," "siren," "alphabet," and "typhoon."…

Being Greek

In the 1950's, only about 30% of Greek adults could read and write. Now, the literacy rate is more than 95%.

An old Greek legend says that when God created the world, he sifted all the soil onto the earth through a strainer. After every country had good soil, he tossed the stones left in the strainer over his shoulder and that is what created Greece.

Greece has more than 2,000 islands, of which approximately 170 are populated. Greece's largest island is the Island of Crete (3,189 sq. miles) (8,260 sq. km.).

Over 40% of the population of Greece lives in the capital Athens (*Athina* in Greek). Since becoming the capital of modern Greece, its population has risen from 10,000 in 1834 to 3.6 million in 2001.

Greece has been continuously inhabited for over 7,000 years.

The Greek civilisation has been around for so long, that some would say, that it has had a chance to try nearly every form of government…

Being Greek

Greece enjoys more than 250 days of sunshine each year which means that they have 3,000 hours of sun every year.

Currently, Greek men must serve from one year to 18 months in a branch of the counties armed forces. The government spends 6% of the annual Gross Domestic Product (GDP) on the military.

Ancient Greece was not a single country like modern Greece. Rather, it was made up of about 1,500 different city-states or *poleis* (singular, *polis*). Each had its own laws and army, and they often quarrelled and waged war on one another. Athens was the largest city-state.

Until the late 1990's, the greatest threat to Greece was Turkey, as the two nations have had historical disputes over Cyprus and other territory for decades. After coming to each other's aid after a devastating earthquake that hit both countries in 1999, their relationship has improved.

Currently the life expectancy for Greek females is 82 years and for men, 77 years. Greece is ranked 26th in the world for life expectancy rates.

Greece is the leading producer of sea sponges in the world…

Being Greek

Greek football supporters, Rethymno and Agia Galini

Football is the national sport of Greece.

Greek merchant ships make up 70% of the European Union's total merchant fleet. According to Greek law, 75% of a ship's crew must be Greek.

Greece has more archaeological museums than any other country in the world.

Retirement homes are rare in Greece. Grandparents usually live with their children's family until they die. Most young people live with their families until they marry.

Many Greek structures such as doors, windowsills, furniture, and church domes are painted a turquoise blue, especially in the Cyclades Islands. It is used because of an ancient belief that this shade of blue keeps evil away.

Feta cheese, which is made from goat's milk is the national cheese of Greece. It dates back to the Homeric ages, and the average per-capita consumption of feta cheese in Greece is the highest in the world…

Being Greek

The Greek City of Rhodes

In Greece, people celebrate the "name day" of the saint that bears their name rather than their own birthday.

Thousands of birds stop in Greece's wetlands on their migrations. As many as 100,000 birds from northern Europe and Asia spend their winters there.

The saying "taking the bull by its horns" comes from the Greek myth of Hercules saving the Island of Crete from a raging bull by seizing its horns.

The City of Rhodes (the capital of the Island of Rhodes) is famous for housing one of the Seven Wonders of the Ancient World: the Colossus of Rhodes (from which the word "colossal" is derived). This gigantic 98-foot (303-meter) statue of the god Helios, whose legs straddled the harbour, unfortunately it was destroyed by an earthquake in 226 B.C.

The first Olympic Games took place in 776 B.C. The first Greek Olympic champion was a Greek cook named Coroebus who won the sprint race…

Being Greek

Slaves made up between 40% and 80% of ancient Greece's population. Slaves were captives from wars, abandoned children, or children of slaves.

A long-standing dispute between Britain and Greece concerns the Elgin Marbles (the Greeks prefer to call them the Parthenon Marbles), which are housed in a London museum. The British government believes that it acquired them fairly through its purchase from Lord Elgin, while the Greeks claim the purchase was illegal as the marbles were the property of the Greek people and therefore, stolen and should be returned to Greece.

Greece has one of the richest diversities of wildlife in Europe, including 116 species of mammals, 18 of amphibians, 59 of reptiles, 240 of bird, and 107 of fish. However, about half of the endemic mammal species are currently in danger of becoming extinct.

The monk seal has been a part of Greek's natural and cultural heritage and is described in **The Odyssey**. The head of a monk seal was even found on a coin dating from 500 BC…

Being Greek

        Alexander the Great   Aristotle

Greece organised the first municipal rubbish/waste dump in the Western World around 500 B.C.

During the Nazi occupation of Greece in WWII, most Jews were taken to concentration camps across Europe. The Jewish population in Greece fell sharply from 78,000 to less than 13,000 by the end of the war.

In Greece, the dead are always buried because the Greek Orthodox Church forbids cremation. Five years after a burial, the body is exhumed and the bones are first washed with wine and then placed in an ossuary. This is done in part to relieve the shortage of land available in Greek cemeteries.

Government corruption cost Greece about $1 billion in 2009. Currently Greece's national debt is larger than the country's economy. Its credit rating, or its perceived ability to repay debts, is the lowest in the euro zone.

The Greek language has been spoken for more than 3,000 years, making it one of the oldest languages in Europe…

Being Greek

Ancient Greek theatre masks

The Greeks do not wave with an open hand. In fact, it is considered an insult to show the palm of the hand with the fingers extended. Greeks wave with their palm closed.

The Greeks after giving a compliment, Greeks make a puff of breath through pursed lips, as if spitting. This is meant to protect the person receiving the compliment from the "evil eye."

No point in Greece is more than 85 miles (137 kilometres) from sea water. Greece has about 9,000 miles of coastline, the 10th longest coastline in the world.

Greece was once a mass of rock that was completely underwater. When a tectonic plate crashed into Europe, the collision raised the sea bed and created Greece's mountain ranges. The plate is still moving and often causes earthquakes and tremors all around the Aegean.

Greek Soldiers (hoplites) in ancient Greece the Greek soldiers wore up to 70 pounds (33 kilograms) of bronze armour…

Being Greek

Socrates

Plato

The first historian in the world is considered to be the Greek writer Herodotus (c. 484-425 B.C.), the author of the first great book of history on the Greco-Persian Wars. Other famous Greeks are Socrates and Plato.

The ancient Greeks are often called the inventors of mathematics because they were the first to make it a theoretical discipline. The work of Greek mathematicians such as Pythagoras, Euclid, Archimedes, and Apollonius lies at the basis of modern mathematics.

The first Greek philosopher is considered to be Thales of Miletus (c. 624-546 B.C.). He was the first to give a natural explanation of the origin of the world rather than a mythological one.

The Peloponnesian War (431-404 B.C.) between Athens and the Peloponnesian League led by Sparta left ancient Greece in ruins and marked the end of the golden age of Greece.

The Greek Spartan specialty was a black soup made from salt, vinegar, and blood. No one else in the rest of Greece would drink it…

Being Greek

Crete Independence Fighters

The British poet Lord Byron (1788-1824) was so enamoured with the Greeks that he travelled to Greece to fight against the Turks in the Greek War of Independence (see above). He contracted a fever there and died at the age of 36. The Greeks consider him a national hero.

The word "barbarian" comes from Greek *barbaroi*, which means people who do not speak Greek and therefore sound like they're saying "bar-bar-bar-bar."

In ancient Greece one of the dishes enjoyed by ancient Greek men at feasts was roast pig stuffed with thrushes, ducks, eggs, and oysters. Most feasts were for men only, though there were female entertainers (this was not considered a respectable occupation for women).

The first Greek tragedy was performed in 534 B.C. and was staged by a priest of Dionysus named Thespis. He also wrote and performed a part separate from the traditional tragic chorus, which also designated him as the first actor. In fact, the word "thespian" (actor) derives from his name…

Being Greek

At its height, Greek colonisation reached as far as Russia and France to the west and Turkey to the east.

Pre-Socratic Greek philosopher Anaximander (c. 610-546 B.C.) is credited with writing the first philosophical treatise and making the first map of the known world. He can also be considered the first scientist who recorded a scientific experiment.

Greek Spartan warriors were known for their long, flowing hair. Before a battle, they would carefully comb it. Cowardly soldiers would have half their hair and half their beards shaved off.

In ancient Greece wealthy people would sacrifice animals at the temples. Poor people who couldn't afford live animals offered pastry ones instead.

Ostracism allowed Athenian citizens to temporarily exile people who were thought dangerous to the public. If it was voted that ostracism was necessary, each citizen inscribed a name on a piece of pottery or ostracon, as it was called, in a secret ballet. The person with the most names had to leave town in 10 days for 10 years…

Being Greek

Greek tragedy actors in their masks

Only Greek boys and men were actors in ancient Greek plays. They wore large masks (see above) so audience members could see what part they were playing. Theatre staff carried big sticks to control the audience because sometimes the huge audiences would get excited by a play and would riot.

The term "Ancient Greece" usually refers to the time between Homer (c. 750 B.C.) and the Roman conquest of Ptolemaic Egypt (Antony and Cleopatra, 30 B.C.).

Greek Democracy in Athens was significantly different from modern democracies in that it was both more participatory and exclusive. There were also no political parties in Athenian democracy.

The Greeks, in ancient times, would sacrifice one hundred bulls to Zeus during each Olympic Games.

The Greeks revolutionised the art of sculpture. Instead of stiff poses and blank faces, Greek artists began to carve statues of people that showed both movement and emotion…

Being Greek

The Greek Gods…

The Greek Temple of Artemis built on the site of two earlier shrines dating back as far as the eight century B.C. in modern-day Turkey, was one of the Seven Wonders of the Ancient World. It was built around 550 B.C. and was destroyed in 356 B.C. by Herostratus.

The Parthenon (see above - Place of the Partheons, from *parthenos* or "virgin") was built almost 2,500 years ago and sits on the Acropolis above the city of Athens. It actually featured colourful sculptures and a large gold-and-ivory statue of Athena. It took 15 years to build.

The ancestors of the Greeks were Indo-Europeans who entered Greece around 1900 B.C. They lived alongside the Minoans for many centuries before giving rise to the Mycenaean civilisation which ended abruptly in the twelfth century B.C. After a "dark ages" of 300 years in which the knowledge of writing was lost, Greece gave birth to one of the most influential civilisation the world has ever known: Classical Greece.

By law, the only people eligible for citizenship in Sparta were direct descendants of the original Doric settlers. Because of this, there were never more than about 6,000-7,000 male citizens in Sparta, compared with up to 40,000 in Athens…

Being Greek

Alexander the Great

The highest elevation in Greece is the legendary home of Zeus and other Olympian gods and goddesses, Mount Olympus at 9,750 feet (2,917 meters). Its lowest elevation is the Mediterranean Sea, or sea level.

Alexander the Great was the first Greek ruler to put his own face on Greek coins. Previously, Greek coins had shown the face of a god or goddess.

The word "tragedy" is Greek for "goat-song" because early Greek tragedies honoured Dionysus, the god of wine, and the players wore goatskins. Tragedies were noble stories of gods, kings, and heroes. Comedy or "revel," on the other hand, were about lower-class characters and their antics.

The most famous modern writer in Greece was Nikos Kazantzakis (1883-1957). His novels **Zorba the Greek** and **The Last Temptation of Christ** were both made into movies, though the Greek Orthodox Church expelled him for writing **The Last Temptation of Christ**.

Greece's official name is the Hellenic Republic. It is also known as Ellas or Ellada…

Being Greek

The Greek flag includes nine blue-and-white horizontal stripes, which some scholars say stand for the nine syllables of the Greek motto *"Eleftheria i Thanatos"* or "Freedom or Death." Blue represents Greece's sea and sky, while white stands for the purity of the struggle of freedom. In the upper left-hand corner is the traditional Greek Orthodox cross.

Greece has two major political parties: the Socialists (Panhellenic Socialists Movements or PASOK) and the Democrats (the New Democracy Party). Both were founded in 1974 after Greece's military dictatorship collapsed.

Greece has one of the lowest divorce rates in the EU. Greece traditionally also has the highest abortion rates.

About 10% of a Greek worker's pay is taken for taxes and another 10% for national health care in return the government provides free hospitals and other medical services.

Greek workers currently get at least 30 days of paid vacation every year…

Being Greek

Cretan fishing boats in Sissi harbour

About 10% of Greek adults are unemployed. Even with a college education, it's hard to find a job in Greece today.

Greece's previous currency, the drachma, was 2,650 years old and Europe's oldest currency. The drachma was replaced with the Euro in 2002.

Throughout history, Greeks have loved the sea. They have more than 1,800 merchant ships in service currently. Greece has one of the largest merchant shipping fleets in the world. Aristotle Onassis and Stavros Niarchos ("The Golden Greek") are some of the best-known Greek shipping businessmen.

When the Roman Empire split in two in A.D. 285, the eastern half, including Greece, became known as the Byzantine Empire. In 1453, Greece fell to the Ottoman Empire. Greece wouldn't achieve independence until 1829.

Greece is the European country with the largest number of newspapers. There are 18 daily newspapers in Athens. Foreign papers can also be found in large cities and on popular holiday Islands…

Being Greek

Cretan roadside shrine

The Electricity supply in Greece is 220 volts AC, 50Hz. Round two-pin plugs are used. North American visitors require a transformer and British visitors an adaptor.

The time in Greece is like most other counties in Europe, Summer (Daylight-Saving) Time is observed in Greece, where the time is shifted forward by 1 hour; 3 hours ahead of Greenwich Mean Time (GMT+3). After the summer months the time in Greece is shifted back by 1 hour to Eastern European Time (EET) or (GMT+2).

In Greece the working hours for Banks and Public Services are from 08.00 to 14.00, Monday to Friday. The shops are usually open Monday-Wednesday- Saturday from 09.00 to 15.00 and Tuesday-Thursday-Friday from 09.00 to 14.00 and 17.00 to 20.00. In these three days of the week, shops close for the siesta at noon and open again in the afternoon. In the tourist areas in high season, most shops stay open all day long, from early in the morning till late in the evening. Shopping Malls in the cities also stay open all day.

Anyone who has visited Greece will be well aware of the numerous small roadside shrines that often contain lit candles and vases of dried flowers. These are erected at sites where loved ones have had a tragic accident, often fatal, accident and their family leave them a light burning to remember them…

Being Greek

Driving in Greece: For those of you that have already sampled the delights of driving on Greek roads you will be familiar with the sometimes unfinished state of the road surface and of the sides of the road and ditches being full of builder's rubble and litter. Beside many of the main roads you will see large advertising boards touting brands of cigarettes, coffee and/or sporting goods.

Greek time: In the summertime, Greece is two hours ahead of the time in the UK (Greenwich meridian time) like elsewhere in Europe. Also in Greece, in the summer season (March – September) you will find that there is something very curious about time. In Greece it is conceived in a very particular way. Here time is not running, there is no such concept of "being on time or late" and a watch is just something to wear. The Greeks themselves are aware of the need for them to take it easy (but not in serving the tourist!) up to the point that G.M.T. is not considered as the Greenwich Meridian Time, but as the Greek Maybe Time! So remember you are on holiday take your time and relax things will get done in the fullness of time or should I say in Greek time.

Greek Religious festivals: Throughout Greece, religious festivals have become a true backbone to many communities. All kinds of festivals and religious feast events take place for example Christian Holy events during Easter, when churches are covered with colourful flowers and bay leaves…

Being Greek

The rosary that most of the Greek men are holding in their hands, sitting outside the kafeneion (cafe in Greece), has no religious meaning, but is only a way of killing time. Try and buy one, it's actually much more difficult to swing it than it looks.

The iron bars sticking out from the flat Greek house roofs are exclusively there for the purpose of a later extension to the house. They have **NOTHING** to do with exemptions from taxpaying, as long as the house isn't yet finished. (It is a good story though)!

Lines on a Greek Olive Tree: On an Olive tree the fact that the trunks of the trees are often painted white (lime-wash) in Greece it is used primarily to fight ants. And besides it looks nice, too!

A single person sitting at a taverna, can wait quite a long time for the waiter to show up. In Greece it's very unlikely that anybody eats alone. He/she must be waiting for someone. For the waiter it will be very impolite and bumptious, to ask for the order before all the guests have arrived. This has changed in the major tourist places, and especially for tourists, but you can still run into this phenomenon in the villages of many places in Greece…

Being Greek

When the Greeks go out for dinner, they always pay cash. NO cheque's and credit cards! And they have always got money enough to pay the bill for their company too. Not being able to pay, would be humiliating beyond belief.

Unfinished buildings is a common sight in Greece. The reason is that Greek people build what they need today and leave the rest of the building unfinished for the future. It may seem that the Greeks are constantly building houses - and they are. Most Greek parents build a house for each daughter, but not for their sons (as they are supposed to marry a girl who will get a house from her parents). Often it is also the daughter that inherits her parents' or grandparents' house when they die.

You might get the impression that Greek men always sit in cafes and drink strong black coffee. They do often go to a kafeneion, but not always, and rarely for a very long time. Often they have a cup of Greek coffee only. Most of them stay there for a short time, just enough to hear what has happened and also to make an appointment with for example the local electrician or the local bricklayer. Of course, Greek women can go to the kafeneion as well, but most of them don't want to, and besides they hear all the gossip from the husband when he comes home. About 20 years ago, you would always find at least two kafenions in a village, no matter how small it was, but painted in different colours. The colours indicated the political party of the owner of the kafenion. This way you avoided political quarrels. Rather practical! It can still be found, but it has become more and more rare as less and less people care about politics in Greece today…

Being Greek

Knossos Palace and Balos beach and Rethymno on Crete

Theft is very, very rare in Greece. It's simply considered too humiliating to steel other people's things or money. On the other hand it's OK to cheat a bit - especially if they don't like the person they cheat.

You will see a Greek priest - or pappas, as they are called - everywhere, as you cannot miss them in their long, black dress and high hat. They are not obliged to wear their priest clothes all the time, but they do, as it is most practical and they are easier to identify this way.

Greek priests can marry and have children, just like in the Lutheran church. But you will never see a woman priest. This is not allowed by the Greek Orthodox Church.

At most Greek beaches you will have to pay for a sun bed and an umbrella (see above). If you think that it is just people trying to get money out of the tourists you're very wrong. It's a job in Greece having a piece of a beach. A man bids for a particular part of the beach each year, and he pays a sum of money, to be allowed to put up his sun beds and umbrellas. During the season it is his responsibility that this part of the beach is kept properly. The price you pay will depend on where the beach is situated, what kind of facilities (taverna, toilets, showers) there are. The tourist police checks that he does his job properly…

Being Greek

If you want to see inside a Greek Church or monastery, you must be properly dressed. It's considered rude to enter a church if your shoulders and knees aren't covered. This rule goes for both men and women. So if you are a tourist and wants to be polite in the country you are visiting then please dress respectfully when visiting a church.

If a Greek invites you out for dinner or a drink, Do Not EVER try to make him "split the bill in half" as we often do here in Northern Europe. I know some tourists who have wanted to be nice to their host for the evening, and they snapped the bill out of his hand and paid it. Never has a friendship been that close to ruin, and the Greek man was more embarrassed than you could ever imagine!

If you are invited to a Greek home, remember to bring something for the hosts. Flowers or chocolate is the most common. If the occasion is a name day, you must bring a present, which you deliver when you enter the house. The present will be put together with the rest of the presents on a table - unopened. The Greeks will open the gifts when all the guests have left. If he or she doesn't like the gift they don't have to pretend and show a lot of gratitude that they really do not feel. Actually it is a very practical habit.

Officially in Greece there is equality between the sexes, but still in Greece today women are often paid less…

Being Greek

About 40 % of the Greek women are engaged in active employment.

Theoretically Greek women are liable for military service, but only volunteers are taking part in the service, and the women seem to be satisfied with this situation.

When divorcing in Greece, all belongings are equally split between the man and woman.

Today a Greek woman may keep her maiden name when marrying if she wants.

Today Greek women only give birth to half as many children, as they did before World War 2. The Greek birth-rate is the second lowest in Europe. Italy has the lowest birth-rate.

Since 1982 it has been legal to have a civil marriage. But today still 95 % of couples are married religiously in the church.

Arranged marriages are forbidden by law. Paying a dowry is illegal too. But still you can see examples of both especially in the remote villages…

Being Greek

The Average Age for Greek women is 82 years. Men live usually until 77 years of age.

Bullet holes in Greek road signs. It is no secret that Greeks own guns, especially in mountainous areas. Road signs are easy targets and you will see many of them that resemble Swiss cheese after suffering some shooting practice. Greeks also usually fire their guns at weddings and other celebrations.

Greek Churches (ekklisies): Large churches are usually found inside the towns but the numerous small ones are practically everywhere. Usually they are white-painted, you will find them on a beach, on the mountain peaks, in deep gorges or inside caves. The people of Greece are deeply religious people and they build churches to express their gratitude to God or to fulfil a "tama", a promise given to God in exchange for a request. The miniature churches next to the roads however, are memorials for people killed in a car accident, at the same spot where the accident happened. The family of the deceased construct and maintain them. They contain a photo of the deceased, some religious objects and a lit candle.

Erotas or Eros, son of Aphrodite, was a god in ancient Greece: It is difficult to give the meaning of the Greek word "erotas" because there is no word for it in English. The closest translation is "being in love". The English word love is "Agapi" in Greek…

Being Greek

Erontas or diktamos is the Greek name for the herb dittany: It used to be a rare, hard to collect herb because it grew on steep cliffs in mountainous areas. Today it is cultivated, so it has become easy to find. It is said that its name "erontas", which is actually the same word as erotas, was given to it because a man should be deeply in love with a woman in order to risk his life to collect it for her from a steep cliff.

Fresh fish in Greece has become rare and quite expensive. Common fish that you will find at restaurants are: red mullet, sea bream, red snapper, swordfish and tuna. Octopus, squids, shrimps and mussels are also easy to find and they taste great. Fish like Sand-Smelt or Silverside are quite cheap and tasty, although its taste is described as "fishy" by people who are not used to Mediterranean fish.

Garides are shrimps: Have them boiled or "saganaki" with tomatoes and feta cheese.

Gazoza, the spirit of the Island of Crete: It is still produced by small companies all over the Island and you will find it at cafes and tavernas in the villages…

Being Greek

Greek Salad: In Greek it is called "horiatiki" and it is a tasty salad made from fresh tomatoes, cucumber, green peppers, olives and feta cheese. Add some oregano, vinegar and plenty of Greek olive oil and you have a tasty and fulfilling dish.

Greek Herbs: If I had to describe Greece in just five words only, then I would choose: sun, sea, mountains, sage and thyme. Sage and thyme are everywhere in Greece and the air is full of their characteristic smell. Herbs have been used since ancient times by the people of Greece as medicines. Try a tea of camomile and sage if you have a sore throat. If you do not like the taste you can add some honey to it. If your nose is blocked and you cannot breathe easily, then have a tea made from thyme.

Greek Honey of excellent quality is produced in Greece. Thyme honey is considered to be the best.

Immigrants into Greece: Albanians, Bulgarians, Russians, Ukranian and others from Eastern Europe have moved to Greece in big numbers. Most of them work in agriculture and construction and their number is more than 10% of the Greek population. They adjusted quickly to the Greek way of life and their children go to Greek schools…

Being Greek

Kafeneio, the Greek café: Is a very important part of the social life of all parts of Greece. They often say that you should always find the time for a coffee.

Lamb meat: The best meat you can have in Greece is the young lamb or young goat meat from animals raised in the mountainous areas. If you happen to be in a taverna in a small mountainous village, ask them for grilled paidakia.

Mizithra: A fresh soft white cheese. It contains lower fat and cholesterol than yellow cheese. It is made from sheep's milk.

Paximadi: The traditional Greek way of preserving bread for a long time. It is hard dried bread that gets soft when you add some water to it. You will find it in various forms, sizes and made from wheat or barley, with or without yeast, whole grain or not. Pour some olive oil on a big round piece of paximadi, add some grated tomato, oregano and feta cheese and you will have the very tasty appetizer.

Pita Giros: are slices of grilled pork meat with yoghurt, lots of onion, French fries, salt and pepper, all wrapped inside a round "pita" bread. Pita - giros is the fast food of Greece and you can find it almost everywhere. Chicken giros is becoming popular lately because of the smaller amount of fat that it contains…

Being Greek

Platanos or Plane Tree: A tree that grows close to water. You can find it usually close to a river in gorges or in the central square of villages in Greece. It looks similar to the maple tree and it can grow very big.

Raki: This is the famous local drink of Crete. It is produced in late October or early November and it is distilled from grape skins. It is transparent, very strong and in the summer it is served cold. Raki is for the Island of Crete what ouzo is for the rest of Greece.

Sariki: Is the traditional head covering for the men of Crete. It is black and is wrapped many times around the top of the head.

Souvlaki: is skewered pork meat, a traditional Greek dish. It is served with French fries and there is also chicken, lamb and swordfish souvlaki.

Cretan Unfinished Houses, is a common sight on the Island of Crete. People in Crete build the frame of their house before their building license expires. Usually people will build a 3-4 floors building. Each floor is meant for just one apartment. They need one apartment for their family but they plan ahead for when their children grow up and have families of their own. They will finish the house later when they need it or they have enough money to do so…

Being Greek

Greek Vegetables: Greece produces many different types of vegetables and they taste a lot better than what you will find in the supermarkets in the rest of Europe. The sea food is great too.

Xanthies: blonde tourist women. Highly appreciated by the "kamakia", the young hot-blooded Greek lovers. Love stories between men of Greece and tourists are common each year. Most of them are just summer love but a few marriages come out of them. The result is that there are many European women living in Greece, mostly German, Dutch and Scandinavian. Be aware though, that having a romantic love affair during your holiday is one thing and living in Greece married to a Greek man is totally different. The cultural differences are many and it is very important not to ignore them.

Zucchini or Courgette: Try zucchini slices deep fried in olive oil. Fried aubergine slices are very tasty too.

Yannis and Yorgos, are the two most common names for men in Greece. Yannis is John and Yorgos is George. More common names are Manolis and Nikos. For women the most common name is Maria.

Now that we understand a bit more about "Being Greek" we will continue our journey once more by going out and about on the beautiful Island of Crete…

Out and About on Crete

Facts About Crete

The name Nisos Kriti is the Greek name for the Island of Crete. Crete is a region of Greece, it is the biggest Island and the most southern one, except for the little Island of Gavdos. Crete is 260 km (160 miles) long and 56 km (35 miles) at its widest point. The area of the Island is 8,260 sq km (3,190 sq mi). The population of the Island of Crete is close to 600,000 people. The population of Greece is 10,665,989 (2003 estimated). The language spoken is Greek and the religion is Greek Orthodox. The currency is the Euro and has been since 2001…

Out and About on Crete

Heraklion City

Rethymnon Town

The Cities and Towns of Crete

On the north coast of Crete is the City of Heraklion (population: 200,000) and the Towns of Chania (population: 80,000) and the Town of Rethymnon (population: 35,000). On the south coast of the Island of Crete are the Towns of Ierapetra, Mires, Timbaki and Paleochora…

Out and About on Crete

Chania Airport on the Island of Crete

Mind your head when coming in to land on the Island of Crete

Airports on Crete

There are five airports on Crete but only three of them are used for passenger flights: the Heraklion airport, the Chania airport in Akrotiri and the Sitia airport. The airports at Kastelli and Timbaki on the Island of Crete are both military airbases…

Out and About on Crete

The harbour at Heraklion

The harbour at Rethymnon

Harbours on Crete

In Crete there are two main large harbours which are the Heraklion harbour and the Souda Bay harbour. The harbours in Rethymnon, Agios Nikolaos and Sitia are much smaller. Along the south coast of Crete there are several small fishing ports and harbours…

Out and About on Crete

Mountains on Crete

Crete is a mountainous Island and the Island's history, as well as the personality of its inhabitants have been greatly affected by these mountains. In the west there is Lefka Ori (White Mountain): 2453 m, in the centre of the Island is Mt Idi (Psiloritis): 2456 m and in the east of the Island there is Mt Dikti: 2148 m. Cretan mountains form a continuous chain from one end of the Island to the other and they make the Island of Crete look much larger than it really is…

Out and About on Crete

The rivers and Kournas lake on Crete

The rivers on the Island of Crete are very short and many dry up in the summer months. The rivers which flow all the year-round are the river at Preveli in southern Rethymnon district and the river at Vrisses in the Chania district. The lake of Kournas, a small but beautiful lake that has tavernas all around its shore is one of the best beauty spots on the Island…

Out and About on Crete

The Islands close to Crete

There are several small Islands that are very close to Crete. Gavdos Island is the furthest point south of Europe and is populated. The Islands of Hrissi or Gaidouronissi, Koufonissi, Dia, Paximadia and Gramvoussa are much smaller and are not populated. Most of them are popular destinations for holidaymakers on a one-day cruise from Crete. The Cyclades Island of Santorini or Thira (see above) is also close to the Island of Crete and there are daily sightseeing cruises for tourist to visit the Island from Crete. We went on one of these cruises to Santorini from Crete and really enjoyed exploring this Island for the day…

Out and About on Crete

Greek flags and the prefectures of Crete

The Administration of the Island of Crete

The Island of Crete is one of the thirteen administrative divisions of Greece. On Crete there are four Nomoi or Prefectures called Chania, Rethymnon, Heraklion and Lassithi and these are sub-divided into many Dimoi (Municipalities). Each Dimoi is made up of various towns and villages…

Out and About on Crete

The economy of Crete

The main sources of wealth on the Island of Crete are agriculture and tourism. The cultivation of the olive tree is very important on Crete and excellent virgin olive oil is produced here. Other important products include oranges, grapes and vegetables from Island smallholding's and commercial greenhouses. The production of honey, cheese and herbs also takes place on the Island and they are all of excellent quality. There is also a large number of sheep and goats being reared on the Island of Crete…

Out and About on Crete

The legacy of the Minoans of Crete

We have already looked at Cretan history which started in about 6000 BC, when the Island was first inhabited but there are some aspects that deserve further coverage. The best known period is the Bronze Age (2600-1100 BC), the period of the Minoan civilisation. During that period Cretans colonised the other Cyclades Islands and in Crete itself the palaces of Knossos, Festos and Zakros were built. The "Big Blue", Minoan ships used to travel and trade all around the Mediterranean Sea. The Minoan cultural influenced the various nations that the Cretans came in contact with which helped give birth to the wider Greek civilisation on the mainland of Greece that we still admire so very much today…

Out and About on Crete

The Geography of the Island of Crete

The north coast of the Island of Crete is the main tourist area and all cities are located there. The southern coast is the ideal place for the tourist who is in search of an isolated beach. Unfortunately as each year passes and their whereabouts become better known, such beaches become a little more difficult to find. Naturism is a common practice on many isolated beaches on the Island. The sea around the Island is crystal clear and clean and is teeming with life. A regular visitor to its waters are loggerhead turtles (see above). The south of the Island is also a good place if you want to train/test yourself in driving on narrow and very winding roads…

Out and About on Crete

The Geography of the Island of Crete

Away from the coastal regions, the interior is a far less well known part of the Island of Crete. This is the mountainous area of Crete; the roads may be really bad, the road signs are of little help and it's hard to find an English speaking person. Here is the place to search for small villages without the familiar "Rent a Room" or "Restaurant" signs being on display. It is the place to meet the local cats and the real Cretans who are a proud and friendly people, with a great sense of humour, ready to help you in any way they can and offer you a glass of "raki" (the locally produced colourless drink – be careful - it is very strong!)…

Out and About on Crete

Greeting the people of Crete

If on your travels you meet a local on the road or in a village taverna just smile and say "kalimera which is good morning", "kalispera that is good evening" or "yasas which means hello". If you ask for some information and want to say thank you, then say "efharisto which is thank you" in Greek…

Out and About on Crete

Who are the people of Crete

A very good description of the people of the Island of Crete was given by the Frankish Bishop of Athens, LPetit: "They are a truly admirable people who learnt to hold on stubbornly throughout the tumultuous events of forty centuries to their native character and local speech. Courage, mingled with an independent spirit that is often close to downright disobedience, a lively wit, vivid imagination, and a language full of images, spontaneous and unaffected, love for every kind of adventure, an indefatigable urge for freedom, that goes hand in hand with an insatiable desire for bravado. Crete is a fertile land that has always given birth to the worthiest of men both in Church and State, in science and in letters, in the economy and in war"…

Out and About on Crete

The Heraklion Archaeological Museum on Crete

The Museum of Heraklion Archaeology is regarded as one of the most important museums in Europe, is located in the centre of Heraklion city. During the Venetian occupation period the Catholic Monastery of Saint Francisco used to be in the same place. Until it's destruction in the earthquake of 1856, it had been one of the richest and most important monasteries in Crete and had contained many great Byzantine frescos. The construction of the Heraklion Archaeological Museum started in the beginning of the 20th century and was completed in 1940. On the ground floor of the museum there are 13 rooms open to the public while on the 1st floor fragments of the original frescos from the Minoan Palace of Knossos are exhibited. All exhibits in the Heraklion Museum come exclusively from archaeological sites on Crete. The exhibits of the museum are arranged chronologically. As soon as the visitors start their tour in the Heraklion Museum they can see the evolution of pottery from the Neolithic period (5000-2500 BC) until the Post-Palace Period (1400- 1100 BC). Worth admiring are the famous Kamares vessels (2000- 1700 BC). A unique exhibit of the Heraklion Archaeological Museum is the clay disc of Phaistos with hieroglyphics and ideograms inscribed on it. Particularly impressive are the figurines of the Minoan Goddesses. These are the famous "Goddesses of the Snakes" because of the snakes they hold. Their dresses offer us valuable clues about the fashion of dress of Minoan women. Other great attractions of the Heraklion Archaeological Museum are the golden jewels found in Minoan burial sites, the mirrors with the ivory handles, the eyebrow hairpins, the ivory hair combs and the swords with golden handles…

Out and About on Crete

The Historical Museum in Heraklion on Crete

The Crete Historical Museum is at 27 Sofokli Venizelou Avenue on the coast road. The Historical Museum is housed in a neoclassical building dating to 1903 which was owned by Andreas Kalokairinos. He granted it to the Society of Cretan Historical Studies to be turned into a museum in 1952. On display are many wonderful things!…

Out and About on Crete

The Historical Museum of Crete…

The Second World War on Crete…

The Historical Museum of Crete in Heraklion

The Historical Museum of Crete houses valuable historical relics of Crete, from the First Byzantine period (330 AD) to World War II that are displayed in its 22 rooms, covering an area of 1,500 square metres. Visitors begin their tour of the Historical Museum in the Andreas G. Kalokairinos Room, which presents an overview of Cretan history via representative exhibits from all the collections and chronological periods. The main exhibit is the 4 x 4 metre model of the city of Chandax (Heraklion) as it was in the mid-17th century, at the peak of its power in Venetian times. Visitors can activate forty different spotlights that pick out the most important monuments of the city…

Out and About on Crete

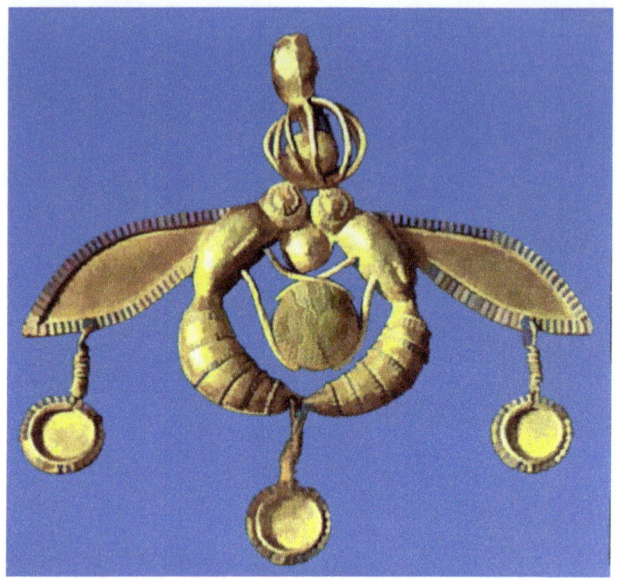

Minoan vase and the Malia Bee brooch

The Chania Archaeological Museum on Crete

The Chania Archaeological Museum is on Halidon Street in the centre of the old town, and houses the Archaeological Collection of the Chania Prefecture. The Archaeological Collection of Chania has been housed in various public buildings (the Residency, the Boys' High School and the Hassan Mosque). Since 1963 it has been housed, albeit temporarily, in the Venetian church of St Francis which once belonged to the Franciscan monks, which is an important monument of the city in its own right. It is not known exactly when the church was built, but written sources refer to it as standing in the great earthquake of 1595 and being the largest building in the city. It was later turned into a Turkish mosque dedicated to Yusuf Pasha, the conqueror of Chania. At the turn of the 20th century it became the "Idaion Andron" Cinema. After the Second World War it was used as a supply depot then in 1963 it became the Archaeological Museum of Chania, a function it has fulfilled ever since…

Out and About on Crete

Minoan Pottery

The Chania Archaeological Museum on Crete

The Chania Archaeological Museum is well worth a visit as it includes finds from the wider Chania area which will give the visitor a good idea of the history of western Crete. The exhibits include pottery, carved stone objects, seal-stones, sculpture, metalwork, gold jewellery and coins that are displayed in chronological order in the cases of the museum. There are also mosaic floors on display from the Roman period (2nd-3rd c. AD), depicting scenes from the Dionysiac cycle and also the myth of Poseidon and of the nymph Amymone. The displays start with Neolithic clay items, then continue with various Minoan objects, rare Geometrical and Hellenistic finds and important Roman items, and ending with objects from the Byzantine period. There is information on the Cretan people's daily lives and lifestyles throughout Cretan history, their burial and other religious rites, their crafts and other occupations. In 2000 the interesting collection of Konstantinos and Marika Mitsotakis was donated to the Archaeological Museum of Chania. The exhibits constitute a third of the whole museum's collection and are presented in chronological order (end of the 4th millennium BC up to the 3rd century AD). Opposite the Archaeological Museum of Chania is a domed building. It is all that remains of a Turkish hamam. Close by was the location of the Chania Jewish community until the outbreak of the Second World War. The Jewish quarter covered the area behind the museum. There were the mansions of eminent Jews, some still preserved today, as well as the synagogue, which has recently reopened. Looking in the same direction, behind the Jewish quarter is the Schiavo Bastion which is part of the Venetian walls which protected Chania many centuries ago…

Out and About on Crete

A Minoan Nobleman…

The Rethymnon Historical and Folk Museum on Crete

The Historical and Folk Museum of Rethymnon in Vernardou Street was founded in 1973 by Christophoros Stavroulakis and Fani Voyiatzaki, who donated the museum building. The building itself is one of the most representative examples of a town house dating from the end of the Venetian occupation (c. 17th century) in the town. The Natural History Museum is located by the sea and has many interesting exhibits. The museum of Rethymnon houses collections of woven fabrics, weaving equipment, embroidery, lacework, pottery, baskets, metalwork, coins, costumes, historical items and much, much more…

Out and About on Crete

The Knossos Minoan Palace on Crete

Knossos, the famous Minoan Palace lies 5 kilometres southeast of Heraklion, in the valley of the river Kairatos. The river rises in Archanes, runs through Knossos and reaches the sea at Katsabas which was the location of the Minoan harbour of Knossos. In Minoan times the river flowed all year round and the surrounding hills were covered in oak and cypress trees, where today we see vines and olives. The pine trees inside the archaeological site were planted by the archaeologist Sir Arthur Evans. Constant habitation of the site for 9,000 years has brought about great changes to the natural environment, so it is hard to imagine what the Minoan landscape was like during their time…

Out and About on Crete

The 1st and 2nd Knossos Minoan Palaces on Crete

The first settlement in the Knossos area was established circa 7000 BC, during the Neolithic Period. The economic, social and political development of the settlement led to the construction of the majestic Palace of Knossos towards the end of the second millennium BC. Knossos was the seat of the legendary King Minos and the main centre of Minoan power on Crete. This first Palace was destroyed circa 1700 BC. It was rebuilt and destroyed again by fire, this time definitively, in 1350 BC. The environs of the Palace were transformed into a sacred grove of the goddess Rhea, but never inhabited again. The Palace of Knossos is the monumental symbol of Minoan civilisation, due to its construction, use of luxury materials, architectural plan, advanced building techniques and its impressive size…

Out and About on Crete

The excavations of the Knossos Minoan Palace on Crete

The first large-scale excavation of Knossos were undertaken in 1878 by the wealthy art-lover Minos Kalokairinos, while Crete was still under Turkish occupation. Kalokairinos excavated part of the West Magazines and brought many large pithoi (storage pots) to light. In March 1900 to 1931, Sir Arthur Evans excavated not only the Palace but the whole surrounding area of Knossos. The Palace complex was excavated in only five years, an extremely short time by today's standards. Evans restored the Palace with concrete, a technique condemned by modern archaeologists as arbitrary and damaging to the Minoan structure. Today excavations continue and a conservation programme is underway to halt any further deterioration of the Palace site…

Out and About on Crete

The Remains of the Minoan Palace at Phaistos on Crete

The Minoan Palace of Phaistos on Crete

The Minoan Palace of Phaistos, is located on the Messara Plain in south-central Crete, 55 kilometres south of Heraklion and a short distance from the archaeological sites of Agia Triada, Gortys and Matala. Phaistos is one of the most important archaeological sites in Crete and attracts many thousands of visitors every year. The Minoan palace of Phaistos which was close to a flourishing city which arose on the fertile plain of the Messara in prehistoric times, from circa 6000 BC to the 1st century BC, as archaeological finds have confirmed. The first palace of Phaistos was built in circa 2000 BC. Its mythical founder was Minos himself and its first King was his brother Radamanthys. In 1700 BC a strong earthquake destroyed the palace, which was then rebuilt almost immediately. However, Phaistos was no longer the administrative centre of the area, an honour which passed to neighbouring Agia Triada. Phaistos continued to be the religious and cult centre of south Crete. In 1450 BC there was another great catastrophe, not only in Phaistos but across the whole of Crete. The city of Phaistos recovered from the destruction, minted its own coins and continued to flourish for the next few centuries until the first century BC, when it was destroyed. The first excavations in the wider area of Phaistos were undertaken in 1900 by the Italian Archaeological School. Most of the buildings visible today on the site belong to the Neopalatial period (1700 - 1450 BC). Unlike Knossos, there has been no restoration undertaken on the site which has only undergone a programme of conservation…

Out and About on Crete

The Minoan Palace of Malia on Crete

Malia is located 37 km east of Heraklion. The sandy beaches and the Sea of Crete are to the north, the mountain of Dikti is to the south, and with a little valley lying between them. The site is 37 km east of Heraklion or 25 Km west of Agios Nikolaos. The Minoan Palace of Malia is the third-largest Minoan palace on Crete, built in a wonderful setting near the sea, on the road linking eastern and central Crete. This palace was the seat, according to myth, of Minos' brother Sarpedon and was first constructed in circa 1900 BC. The already large settlement, some parts of which are preserved around the palace, thus became a Minoan Palace City State. This first palace on the site was destroyed circa 1700 BC and rebuilt circa 1650 BC, on the same site and with the same layout. The new palace was destroyed circa 1450 BC and the site was not reoccupied during the Mycenean period apart from a small building, probably a sanctuary that was constructed in the ruins. Most of the ruins visible today belong to the Neopalatial complex which was the second palace built on the site. The majestic size, complex plan and multiple details of the palace make it a fascinating place to visit…

Out and About on Crete

The Remains of the Minoan Palace of Zakros on Crete

The Minoan Palace of Zakros on Crete

The Minoan Palace of Zakros on Crete is situated on Crete's eastern coast, in the region of Zakros, just south of Palaikastro which is another interesting Minoan settlement. Of the four Minoan palaces to be discovered by archaeologists the palace of Zakros is the smallest. Zakros Palace is only a fifth of the size of Knossos, the latter being the largest of the Minoan palaces on Crete and the centre of the Minoan civilisation on the Island. The first excavations in the area occupied by Zakros Palace were done in the early 1900's. They were headed by David George Hogarth, an archaeologist and scholar who worked with the British School of Archaeology in Athens. Hogarth's digs yielded about 10 Late Minoan houses and other valuable findings such as pottery, bronze tools and spurs. The ruins of Zakros Palace emerged when work at the site was resumed after the Second World War by renowned Greek archaeologist Nikolaos Platon in 1961. The excavations at Kato Zakros are still ongoing. The historical Minoan items un-earthed in Zakros Palace are considered to be some of the most important discoveries made to-date. Because the Zakros Minoan palace was unearthed a lot later than the other three of its kind, the work done here made use of more advanced methods in archaeology. But more than that, the ruins of Zakros Palace had been preserved over time because they had not been plundered by robbers…

Out and About on Crete

The Crete City of Gortys or Gortyn or Gortyna

Gortys, also known as Gortyn or Gortyna is one of the most important cities on Crete with an unbroken history of 6,000 years and is one of the most extensive archaeological sites in Greece. It lies in south central Crete in the fertile Mesara plain, the site of the first human habitation of Crete at the end of the Neolithic period (5th millennium BC). Gortys is about 40 minutes' drive south of Heraklion, on the same road that goes to Phaistos and Matala. Gortys is about 1 km past the village of Agii Deka. According to one tradition, Gortys was named after its founder Gortys, the son of Radamanthys, King of Phaistos and brother of King Minos. Gortys was one of the first areas of Crete to attract the attention of researchers and archaeologists as early as the period of Turkish occupation in the late 19th century, when Minoan civilisation was still a matter of conjecture and myth. In 1884 the discovery and preservation of the Great Inscription led to excavations in the Gortys area that lasted until 1940. A large part of the Roman city still remains unexplored today…

Out and About on Crete

History of the Crete City of Gortys

The area around Gortys has been inhabited since the end of the Neolithic period and continued into Minoan times, a fact proven by the Minoan country villa found in the Kannia area near Mitropolis village, not far from Gortys. From the middle of the 1st millennium BC, Gortys replaced Phaistos as the chief power in the area with its fortified acropolis and its temple of Athena Poliouchos (Protector of the City). After the Roman conquest of Crete in 67 BC, Gortys, which was well disposed towards Rome, became capital of Crete, replacing Knossos. Gortys was declared the capital of the Roman province of Crete and Cyrenaica, a position it held until the Arab conquest of Crete in 828 AD. Gortys reached the peak of its power in the 2nd century AD, while its final period of glory was in the early Christian period (until the 7th century AD). In 796 AD the city was hit by an earthquake which almost destroyed it. After the Andalusian Arabs conquered Crete in 828 AD, the capital was transferred to Chandax, modern-day Heraklion…

Out and About on Crete

The Greek God Zeus...

The Ideon Cave or Ideon Andron on Crete

The Ideon Cave or Ideon Andron is found on Mt Ida or Psiloritis, the highest mountain in Crete. The Ideon Cave is one of the greatest cave sanctuaries in Crete and is as important as the major Greek temples. It flourished in antiquity (4000 BC to the 1st century AD). The Ideon Cave was famous for being the place where Zeus, the Father of the Mythological Greek Gods, was born and grew up. This claim is contested by some people who say that the Dikteon Cave in East Crete was the birthplace of Zeus. The Ideon Cave is on the east side of Mount Ida in central Crete, at an altitude of 1,498 metres. The cave is 20 kilometres after the village of Anogia and a few metres higher than the Nida Plateau. Legend has it that Mount Ida has the privilege of seeing the sun before the dawn. It is true that on clear days you can see almost the whole of Crete from here, as well as the Cyclades and even Mount Taygetus on the mainland in the Peloponnese region of Greece…

Out and About on Crete

The Ideon Cave and the Myth of the Birth of the Greek God Zeus

In Greek Mythology the son of Cronus and Rhea would overthrow his father, who defended his position by devouring his children. The mother Rhea, however, could not bear this, so she tricked her husband and gave him a rock wrapped in swaddling clothes to swallow instead of her last-born son. After Zeus was born she hid the infant deep in a cave where he was nursed by the nymph Melissa and the goat Amalthea, whose horn produced all manner of good things. The baby's cries were covered by the legendary Curetes, who beat drums and clashed their shields as they danced. Thus the prophecy came true, and when Zeus came of age he overthrew his father Cronus and claimed his power. In days gone by festivals were held at the Ideon Cave each year, originally in honour of the god of vegetation, who died and was reborn in the cycle of the seasons. The Minoan god of vegetation was later replaced by the Cretan-born Zeus, the local young Zeus, who according to local myth also died and was reborn each year. During the ceremonies, worshippers hung offerings from the branches of a poplar tree in front of the entrance to the cave. Even Minos, the legendary King of Crete, came on pilgrimage to the Ideon sanctuary every nine years to receive the renewed laws from his father Zeus…

Out and About on Crete

Fortezza, the Venetian Fortress in Rethymnon on Crete

The Fortezza is the Venetian fortress of Rethymnon which is located almost in the centre of the old town. The giant Fortezza, with its hidden centuries of history, is visible from every corner of the town and offers panoramic views of Rethymnon and the coast of Crete to the west. According to one theory, the hill on which the Fortezza is built was once, in a time lost in the mists of history, an Island joined to Crete by a narrow strip of land. Over the centuries the channel silted up and the hill became part of the Cretan mainland. The hill of Paleokastro ("Old Castle") was probably the site of the acropolis of ancient Rithymna with its Temple of Apollo and Sanctuary of Artemis, although this has not been proven to date. In the 3rd century AD, in the Roman period, there is a reference to a temple of Artemis Roccaea on the hill. In those times Rethymnon was an independent city with its own coinage…

Out and About on Crete

Fortezza, the Venetian Fortress in Rethymnon on Crete

During the Second Byzantine Period (10th-13th c. AD), a small walled settlement was established east of Paleokastro hill, the Castrum Rethemi or Castel Vecchio or Antico Castello ("Old Castle") as the Venetians later called it. In the early 13th century the Genoese pirate Enrico Pescatore, an enemy of the Venetians who claimed Crete for himself, seems to have repaired the Byzantine fortifications surrounding the buildings of the small town near the harbour. The Castrum Rethemi was preserved after the Venetian occupation of the Island in the 13th century, but unfortunately nothing remains today of the fortifications with their square towers and two gates. Much later the local authorities, both Venetian and Cretan, the people of Rethymnon and the Venetian Senate, decided to build a fortress which could shelter all the houses in Rethymnon. The hill of Paleokastro was chosen as the most suitable site and work began on the Fortezza, one of the largest and most complete fortification works built in Crete under Venetian rule…

Out and About on Crete

Fortezza, the Venetian Fortress in Rethymnon on Crete

The Fortezza was built according to the bastion fortification system, with bastions joined by straight sections of thick curtain wall, inclined outwards to make enemy missiles bounce off without damaging the fortress. The foundation stone of the Fortezza was laid on the 13 September 1573. Work on the walls and the public buildings within them was completed by 1580. During the years it was being built, 107,142 Cretans took part in compulsory labour and 40,205 pack animals were requisitioned to work on the Fortezza. As soon as the Fortezza was completed it became obvious that there was hardly any space left for private homes, so the fortress was declared a public area, only to be used as a last resort by the inhabitants in the event of a siege. The Fortezza was never a particularly secure fortress and had various flaws, such as the lack of a ditch (the outer burgh, the area just outside the walls of the Fortezza, was a residential zone) or buttresses (the walls were low, without sufficient support), making the fortress easy to scale with ladders. All in all it was not a very good stronghold…

Out and About on Crete

Fortezza, the Venetian Fortress in Rethymnon on Crete

At the turn of the 20th century almost the whole of the interior of the Fortezza was full of residential buildings. Immediately after the Second World War, however, the inhabitants of the Fortezza began to move out to other parts of Rethymnon. Inside the Fortezza all of the ruined buildings, mostly houses, were demolished which destroyed any remaining traces of the Turkish period. The constant and varied use of the Fortezza over the centuries altered its original form both internally and externally. It took about twenty years to repair the damage to the fortress and remove the brothels of Rethymnon established there. It is worth noting that for a long time the Fortezza even housed the local prison. Today the outer fortifications of the Fortezza are preserved intact and some buildings are still being restored, allowing visitors to gain a good impression of life in the Fortezza in Venetian times. Having explored the Island we will, in the next chapter, stay outside and visit the best beaches on the Island of Crete…

The Best Beaches on Crete

Balos Beach

Balos is among one of the best beaches in Greece and one of the most beautiful beaches on the Island of Crete. It is 60 km North West of Chania Town. It is seen as a lagoon from the hills above the beach. Balos has white sand, soft sandy seabed and crystal clear seawater. Opposite the sandy beach, there is a rocky Island called Gramvoussa and on top of this Island, there is a Venetian castle that give the visitor gorgeous views of the surrounding area and out to sea. Balos beach is down a rough track that comes from Kaliviani, a village close to Kissamos. This track is about 10 km long and is best travelled by using a 4-wheel drive car. Otherwise, visitors can sail to the beach by using an excursion boat from Kissamos…

The Best Beaches on Crete

Elafonisi Islet

Elafonisi (or Elafonissos) is a small islet connected to the rest of Crete by a shallow reef that can be crossed when the sea is calm. This islet lies 82 km northwest of Chania town and can be reached by boat or by car. Elafonisi (Island of Deer) is like a paradise on earth, and has a wonderful beach with pink coral sand and crystalline seawater. This magical place was almost deserted for a long time but now it has become a popular place to visit and can get pretty crowded during the summer season. Only a couple of tavernas are near the beach. There is no accommodation on the Islet, but camping is allowed…

The Best Beaches on Crete

Vai Lassithi Beach

The beautiful Vai Lassithi beach, known as Palm Forest, is located 25 km east of Sitia and 94 km east of Agios Nikolaos town. It is the only indigenous wild date palm grove in Greece, extending over an area of 250 square kilometres and consists of 5000 palm trees which make it the largest known palm tree forest throughout Europe. This forest was first mentioned during the Classical period and its existence is attributed to Phoenician merchants who threw away the seeds of the dates they were eating. In front of this unique forest, kilometres of pure and soft golden sand extend, boarded by an azure blue sea. The magic and tropical aspect of the place attracts thousands of visitors which makes it very crowded during the summer season. The main beach is open from sunrise to sunset. Open fires and camping is prohibited in the area. Snack bars are located on the beach…

The Best Beaches on Crete

Falassarna Beach

Falassarna is one of the best beaches on Crete and is located in a beautiful fertile plain near the village of Platanos and 58 km west of Chania Town. It consists of pure and soft golden sand and incredibly clean turquoise seawater. Some umbrellas and sun beds can be found on the beach. Falassarna beach is truly an idyllic and quiet place to relax in. It has one of the cleanest beaches in the whole of Greece. During windy days it is better to avoid swimming. From the beach the view is astonishing and the sunsets are really magical. A few good taverns can be found in the surrounding area…

The Best Beaches on Crete

Preveli Beach

The beach of Preveli is situated 40 km south of the main Town and is one of the most idyllic beaches in the Rethymno area. Preveli beach reminds visitors of an exotic lagoon. It is an oasis of palm trees with crystalline greenish seawater and fine soft golden sand. The Kourtaliotis River ends at this wonderful beach, creating a delta. Apart from the superb palm trees, lush vegetation surrounds the beach and the river, creating a dreamy landscape. Because of its extreme beauty, the Preveli Beach unfortunately, as you would expect, gets very crowded during the summer. This wonderful place can be reached by walking from the nearby Preveli Monastery or by boarding one of the fishing boat trips which leave regularly from the ports of Plakias and Agia Galini that visits the beach…

The Best Beaches on Crete

Matala Beach

Matala is one of the most famous beaches in Greece and is located 67 km south west of Heraklion Town. The beach has light golden sand, sunbeds and umbrellas available for hire. On the right side of the beach are the famous imposing cliffs that have the curved caves in that hippies used as shelters/homes in the 1960's. Equally important is the fact that the beach was actually inhabited during Antiquity when the locals actually dug these caves into the cliffs. Today, the prehistoric caves are fenced off. Matala was a fishing village in the past but today locals are mostly engaged in tourism. Matala has some really good fish tavernas and a camping site nearby…

The Best Beaches on Crete

Rodakino Village

The small village of Rodakino (word meaning peach in Greek) is situated 43 km south of Rethymno Town and close to Plakias village. There are some very good beaches nearby. It is an ideal place for relaxing in and watching the world go by. All the nearby beaches are quite isolated and have no facilities or other amenities. The beaches are all very isolated and therefore, offer the visitor a calm and peaceful atmosphere. Other small secluded beaches can be found on the road linking Rodakino to Plakias...

The Best Beaches on Crete

The Plakias World War II Monument

Plakias Beach

Plakias beach is located 40 km south of Rethymno Town. It is a beautiful sandy beach with wonderful clean seawater and sun beds, umbrellas, various water sports, tavernas, cafes and good restaurants all of which makes this a popular resort beach during the summer months. Also there is a war monument to the fallen and to the brave Cretan resistance fighters of World War 11 which overlooks the sea above the beach. In the nearby resort visitors will be able to find good accommodations, shops and family entertainment…

The Best Beaches on Crete

Tymbaki Beach

Tymbaki is a small sand and pebble beach about 70 km south west of Heraklion and close to Tymbaki village. The beach is also known as Kokkinos Pyrgos. There is a small harbour by the beach where boats moor. Tymbaki beach is not as popular with sunbathers as the nearby Matala and Agia Galini beaches as it can often be affected by strong winds that create some big waves that are good for those who like watersports. The beach is very quiet and clean. There is a good choice of accommodation close to the beach and some good quality traditional tavernas…

The Best Beaches on Crete

Istro Beach

On the coastal road south of Agios Nikolaos there are five or six beaches between Agios Nikolaos and Mohlos. One of them is called Istro beach which is 12 km south of Agios Nikolaos Town on the road towards Ierapetra. The crystal clear blue seawater and the white sandy beach are two of the main reasons that make this beach very popular with visitors. It is surrounded by green slopes covered with vegetation. There are sunbeds and umbrellas and some great tavernas that specialise in Cretan cuisine and fresh seafood. Istro beach is very quiet, peaceful and is therefore, ideal for a relaxing beach holiday destination…

The Best Beaches on Crete

Useful Information when using Cretan beaches

No shark attacks have ever been reported in the seas around Crete. Whilst it is true that there are sharks in the Mediterranean they do not approach the shore. You are also safe from jellyfish (see above) stings on most of the Cretan beaches, as the strong currents offshore keep them away from the shoreline. There are not many dangerous fish or sea creatures in the sea around Crete apart from Scorpion fish (which live on rocky sea bottoms) and Weaver fish (which live on sandy sea bottoms) which have a painful sting, but are harmless to humans unless you are allergic. Sea urchins are a threat to your feet on rocky shores. Enter the sea carefully and wear footwear whenever possible. You are unlikely to see dolphins off any Cretan beach because unfortunately they prefer to swim in deep water and rarely approach the shoreline however, you may see dolphins if you take a boat trip during your stay on the Island as they like to swim beside the wakes of boats for fun…

The Best Beaches on Crete

Beautiful Chania on Crete

Useful Information when using Cretan beaches

Naturism on the Island of Crete is not officially allowed but it is however, tolerated on secluded beaches. You will have to use your judgement as to whether you can practise naturism or not on a specific beach. If there are other naturists there, then it is unlikely to be a problem. However the situation changes all the time. A beach may be clothing optional during the week but at weekends it may be occupied by locals so clothing must be worn. Respect their customs and avoid practising naturism in these circumstances…

The Best Beaches on Crete

Agia Galini, a lizard, Daios, Elounda, Gournes and Heraklion

Useful Information when using Cretan beaches

When you are on holiday remember to take your sunscreen, sunglasses, a hat and plenty of drinking water, especially if you plan to visit some secluded beach along the southern coast of the Island of Crete. People on medication should check with their doctor for potential sunbathing risks and follow their advice. Remember to also take any medication with you that you may need during your stay. People should remember that alcohol and swimming are not compatible and can lead to serious medical situations and remember that responsible drinking is a must whilst on the beach or in the sea. Always remember to leave nothing behind on the beach when you leave except your footprints…

The Best Beaches on Crete

Kato Zakros, Iraklio, Hersonissos and Kalamaki

Useful Information when using Cretan beaches

The sea around the Island of Crete is warm in summer and swimming is always a pleasant experience. The seawater temperature is 20 C in May, rising to 26-27 C in July and gradually falling back to 20 C in November. Even in winter the seawater temperature does not often fall below 17 C, so if you are a hardy soul, you can swim in the sea off Crete all the year round. The beaches along the north coast of Crete are usually shallower and the seawater is slightly warmer. There are also lifeguards during the summer on most north coast beaches. The beaches along the south coast are less crowded. You may notice that some of the beaches have campers on them but officially camping is not allowed outside approved campsites. The police may ask you to leave. Hiring sunbeds and umbrellas, can sometimes be costly for a family, but on most beaches there is usually some free beach space that will allow the visitors to lay down directly onto their towels on the warm sand if they wish. This space can also be used by the children (adults) for building their sand castles on…

The Best Beaches on Crete

Kalives, Limenas and Loutraki

Useful Information when using Cretan beaches

Strong winds can blow all year round onto the coast of the Island of Crete. Depending on the time of year, there are often strong southerly winds (in winter) or northerlies (all of the year round). In summer there are also the Meltemia or Etesian winds. These are seasonal north westerlies that are common across the southern Aegean Sea. The winds start up at around 10am in the morning and die down again at dusk. The wind has a different effect on Crete beaches depending on whether these are on the north or the south coast of the Island. On the North coast of Crete the north winds create high waves. This may prove dangerous for inexperienced swimmers. Be careful and always follow the lifeguards' instructions and be safe…

The Best Beaches on Crete

Loutro, Marathi and Palekastro

Useful Information when using Cretan beaches

On the south coast of the Island of Crete the north winds blow from the land out to the sea. The sea remains calm but the sand carried by the wind can hit your body and make you feel like someone is trying to sandblast the skin off your body. This happens on a few days each year when the north winds are particularly strong, mainly in July and August so on these day it may be a good idea to visit somewhere inland or visit one of the following beaches: The beaches on the Island that are largely unaffected by the wind are: Marathi, Kalyves, Almyrida, Plaka, Bali, Agia Palagia, the Limanaki, Loutra, Kali Lameness, Arvi, Myrtos and Makrygialos…

The Best Beaches on Crete

Rethymno, Sissi, Stalos, Vai and Spinalonga Island

Useful Information when using Cretan beaches

Dogs have the right to come onto the beaches on the Island of Crete, unless there is a Municipal or Prefectural sign displayed indicating otherwise. According to Law you can walk a dog in any outdoor areas (i.e. including beaches) as long as it is on a lead and that you clean up after it. You should also carry the dogs health book with you to prove it has been vaccinated. Dogs may not swim on busy beaches on pain of a fine. However this does not apply to remote beaches, even if there are people swimming there. Having enjoyed our time on the beach it is now time, In the next chapter, to enjoy the beautiful Island of Crete in full colour...

Crete in Colour

The beautiful Island of Crete

Crete in Colour

The beautiful Island of Crete

Crete in Colour

The beautiful Island of Crete

Crete in Colour

The beautiful Island of Crete

Crete in Colour

The beautiful Island of Crete

Crete in Colour

The beautiful Island of Crete

Crete in Colour

The beautiful Island of Crete

Crete in Colour

The beautiful Island of Crete

Crete in Colour

The beautiful Island of Crete

Crete in Colour

The beautiful Island of Crete

Crete in Colour

The beautiful Island of Crete

Crete in Colour

The beautiful Island of Crete

Crete in Colour

The beautiful Island of Crete

Crete in Colour

The beautiful Island of Crete

Crete in Colour

The beautiful Island of Crete

Crete in Colour

The beautiful Island of Crete

Crete in Colour

The beautiful Island of Crete

Crete in Colour

The beautiful Island of Crete

Crete in Colour

The beautiful Island of Crete

Crete in Colour

The beautiful Island of Crete

Crete in Colour

The beautiful Island of Crete

Crete in Colour

The beautiful Island of Crete

Crete in Colour

The beautiful Island of Crete

Crete in Colour

The beautiful Island of Crete

Crete in Colour

The beautiful Island of Crete

Crete in Colour

The beautiful Island of Crete

Crete in Colour

The beautiful Island of Crete

Crete in Colour

The beautiful Island of Crete

Crete in Colour

Now that we have enjoyed some of the colourful scenery on the Island of Crete it is time for us to board a boat and sail off into the sunset to visit the Paradise Greek Island of Santorini…

The Island of **Santorini**

Exploring the Island of Santorini

While on holiday on the Island of Crete we went on a boat trip to explore the rich history and stunning beauty of the Island of Santorini. We left from our hotel very early one morning and after leaving the capitals harbour by boat we arrived at the Island of Santorini by mid-morning…

The Island of Santorini

Exploring the Island of Santorini

Our first impression was of awe as we arrived at Santorini. We had the sheer high cliffs that confronted our boat and the wonderful circular bay that we found ourselves in was amazing to behold! We journeyed up to the village perched on top of the cliffs up steep steps on the backs of donkeys. After a period of shopping and sightseeing we had a cold drink before venturing onto the sea once more to visit first the volcanic island in the bay before visiting the Minoan City of Akrotiri which was destroyed and engulfed by the volcano so long ago. In the following pages we explore the history of this wonderful and historic Island and ask the question: **Was this really the fabled Lost Kingdom of Atlantis?**…

The Island of Santorini

Exploring the Island of Santorini

In ancient times, the Island of Santorini was called Thera. It took its present name from the Venetians in the middle Ages (Saint Irene- Santorini). In antiquity, the Island had times of great prosperity and times of decline. The site of Ancient Thera is perched on a hill called Messa Vouno high above Perissa Beach, on the south-eastern coast of the Island. This town originally was a religious centre due to its high location and its marvellous views…

The Island of Santorini

Exploring the Island of Santorini

The first traces of human inhabitancy on Ancient Thera was in the Neolithic Period. There was several scattered settlements, mainly close to Akrotiri that witnessed human activity until the middle of the 16th century BC when a strong volcanic eruption destroyed the entire human settlement leaving no traces. Since then, Thera remained deserted for centuries until written sources mention Santorini in the Peloponnesian War of 431 BC and again during the Roman Empire...

The Island of Santorini

The Greek Gods…

Exploring the Island of Santorini

Ancient Thera became prosperous and populated again during the Hellenistic Period, as witnessed by the remains of cemeteries and numerous places of worship. Through this prosperous period, Thera developed and the agora (meeting place) was expanded and numerous other buildings were constructed. At the same time, places of worship were added and sanctuaries to honour the Greek Gods and Kings. The houses of the people were richly decorated. After the 3rd century AD, the town of Ancient Thera declined once more. Several excavations in the early 20th century have revealed parts of the old town. The items discovered are today housed in the Museum of Prehistoric Thera in Fira on Santorini…

The Island of Santorini

Exploring the Island of Santorini

Archeological excavations on Santorini have established that the Island of Santorini had an important civilisation on it in around 3600 BC. Excavations discovered an important city near Akrotiri and close to the famous red beach that proved the existence of an ancient Minoan colony on the Island. The city was very similar to those found on the Island of Crete. It had many wall ornaments, paintings and pottery showing naturalistic landscapes of animals and humans in the ancient Minoan style. The Minoan city of Akrotiri and all life on the Island was destroyed and engulfed by a volcanic eruption in the distant past…

The Island of Santorini

Exploring the Island of Santorini

In Ancient times, Santorini Island was known as Stongili, which means round in Greek. Stongili was the victim of an enormous volcanic eruption in 1,500 BC. The eruption was so huge that many consider it to be the main cause of the destruction of the great Minoan civilisation not just on Santorini but on the Island of Crete which is situated 70 nautical miles away. The specialists believe that the explosion was so powerful that it created gigantic waves that reached the shores of the surrounding Islands and Crete itself. After the explosion, the centre of Santorini sank, and the many earthquakes that followed destroyed a large part of the rest of the Island. When the dust settled the Minoans were gone forever!…

The Island of **Santorini**

Exploring the Island of Santorini

In some ancient myths, the destruction of the Island of Santorini is closely associated to the legend of Atlantis. According to history the Phoenicians settled on ancient Thera around 1,300 BC and stayed for five generations. Then, around 1100 BC, the Island was occupied by the Lacedaemonian. Around 825 BC, the inhabitants of the Island, then named Thera, were using the Phoenician alphabet. In the 7th and 6th centuries BC, Thera had commercial and trade relations with most of the Islands and cities of Greece. During the Hellenistic Period, Thera, because of its central position in the Aegean, became an important trade centre and an important naval base, due to its strategically perfect position…

The Island of Santorini

Sailing to Santorini

Exploring the Island of Santorini

The Destruction of the Minoan Civilisation: The Minoan Civilisation flourished more than 5000 years ago. Since the first archaeological pick axe unearthed the tantalising signs of the Minoan Palace at Knossos, almost 100 years ago, the cause of the destruction of the Minoan Civilisation has been the subject of much controversy, debate and dispute among scientists. They do however, agree that the Minoan Civilisation was a Bronze Age civilisation that arose on Crete and flourished almost 5000 years ago, until it was destroyed in 1450 BC by the volcanic eruption of the Minoan Island of Thera (Santorini)…

The Island of Santorini

Exploring the Island of Santorini

The Minoans were an enigmatic people; educated, warriors and merchants, artists, and experienced sailors. As a result their maritime empire was vast. The Minoan were the first in Europe to use a written language, referred to as Linear A, which was finally decoded just a few years ago. They were different than the mainland Greeks and dominated the Mediterranean Sea, especially since they were not menaced by external forces from the Greek mainland or elsewhere. All of a sudden though, at the height of its power, the Minoan Civilisation was destroyed and perished forever, leaving important examples and tokens of its grandeur. The inexplicable end of this civilisation made many archaeologists to associate its demise with the eruption of the Santorini (Thera) Volcano…

The Island of **Santorini**

Exploring the Island of Santorini

Is Crete or Santorini the lost Atlantis? Many scientists and archaeologists associate Minoan Crete with the lost Atlantis, partially when considering the words of Plato, whose descriptions fit the findings and evidence of the Minoan Civilisation. Since Plato described the story of Atlantis, numerous myths, legends, and scientific studies have appeared. Many people believe that Atlantis is located in maybe Crete, or Santorini. Or maybe, Atlantis is just a myth. In any case even today this story fascinates and intrigues numerous people all over the world…

The Island of Santorini

Exploring the Island of Santorini

The Eruption of the Santorini Volcano and the destruction of the Minoan Civilisation. Somewhere between history and myth lie two historical events of immense importance that shook up and overwhelmed the ancients. These were the destruction of the Minoan Civilisation and the eruption of the Santorini Volcano, almost 3,500 years ago. Since Sir Arthur Evans discovered the lost Palace of King Minos in Knossos on the Island of Crete, archaeologists and scientists have been trying to connect the two events…

The Island of Santorini

Exploring the Island of Santorini

The predominant theory regarding the destruction of the Minoan Civilisation has been for years that it was provoked by something as violent and as sudden as the eruption of the Santorini Volcano. Originally it was believed that the eruption took place in 1450 BC, when the Minoan Civilization perished, but the latest findings and theories puts the event at somewhere between 1627 BC and 1600 BC. The cosmogonic event of the eruption has perplexed historians for years. Today, the scientific world is trying to explain and reconstruct the sequence of events that lead to the destruction of the Island of Thira (Santorini) and probably devastated the whole Minoan Civilisation. It is true that the Volcanic ash from the Santorini Volcano covered Akrotiri on Thira and reached the Cretan shores. Was it enough to wipe off the World map the Minoans. I think so but who really knows?

The Island of Santorini

The Volcano on Thera

Exploring the Island of Santorini

Was the Minoan Civilisation destroyed by the mass eruption of the Thera volcano and the subsequent tsunamis? For many years, the views and theories of archaeologists have diverged. Relatively recently though, new discoveries in Palaikastro on Crete that gives us enough hints of a plausible explanation. Archaeologists have suggested that the volcanic ash from Santorini obviously shadowed Crete for a few days, but in their view, that under no circumstances did it destroy the Minoan Civilisation. So we are still left wondering why did this wonderful and advanced culture vanish…

The Island of **Santorini**

The Minoans on the Island of Thera (Santorini is this Atlantis?)

Exploring the Island of Santorini

The experts have recently found on Crete deposits of stone and pottery, in pieces or powered, and lots of lumps of volcanic ash. They also discovered foraminifera, tiny marine organisms, usually found only on the seabed, and coralline algae, elements that cannot be seen on the mainland. The only way they could have been deposited on the land of Crete was by a tsunami. The tidal wave caused by Santorini Volcano travelled and hit the shores of Crete, destroying the plantations, the crops, the ships and commerce, de-vitalising and destroying the Minoan Civilisation. It was discovered that the Minoan ports on Crete and there infrastructures were totally destroyed by the 50 feet waves and were never rebuilt. The scientist's conclusions was horrifying: not only one, but several successive tsunamis, of more than 50 feet were hitting the Cretan shores, every thirty minutes. Minoans could not have known what fate had written for them. We can only just imagine the terror; these people had experienced they may have been able to run away, maybe some of them returned back to help the wounded or find family members only to see more huge waves coming at them. This was something that happened over and over again, destroying completely the Minoan settlements on Santorini and on the northern and eastern shores of the Island of Crete…

The Island of Santorini

The Volcano on Santorini Today

Exploring the Island of Santorini

Experts now believe that an invasion by the mainland Greek Mycenaeans of Crete and Santorini led to the final complete destruction of the Minoan Civilisation. Archaeologists have now enough evidence to believe that the Minoan Civilisation was severely damaged and affected by the eruption of the Santorini Volcano, which destroyed their fleet. Prosperity and the safety of the Minoan people heavily relied on their ships to provide wealth and security. As their main means of existence and defence had been destroyed by the eruption and subsequent tsunamis the Minoans became an easy prey for the Mycenaean invaders that came to the Island of Crete and Santorini from the Greek Mainland. The Minoans did not disappear overnight and many years passed until the Minoan Civilisation was completely destroyed. It is estimated that the palaces of the Minoan Civilisation were destroyed almost 150 years after the volcanic eruption. Even if we never discover if Plato's words were allegoric or prophetic, or if Atlantis ever really existed, the studies and combinations of evidences gives us a satisfactory and realistic answer to the reasons for the down-fall of one of the most important European Civilisations of antiquity the Minoan…

The Island of **Santorini**

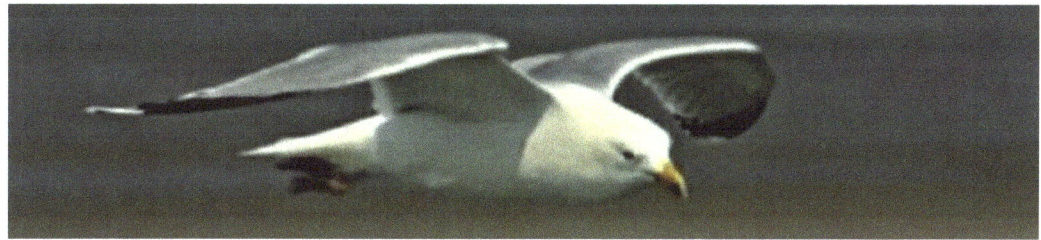

Exploring the Island of Santorini

In the modern era between 1200 and 1579, the Island of Santorini was under Byzantine rule and the church of Episkopi Gonia was founded. In 1204 the Island is surrendered to the Venetian Marco Sanudo and becomes part of the Duke of the Aegean. The name of the Island was given by the Venetians after the Santa Irini, the name of a catholic church. During Turkish rule (1579-1821) the Island succeeds in trading with the ports of the Eastern Mediterranean. The period that followed was quite prosperous. Due to the wars of the 20th century, Santorini's economy declined and the inhabitants abandon the Island after the catastrophic earthquake of 1956. The tourist development on Santorini began in the 1970's and today it is without doubt one of the best tourist destinations in the World…

The Island of Santorini

Exploring the Island of Santorini

In summary the Island of Santorini consists of a semicircular archipelago of volcanic Islands located in the southern Aegean Sea, between the Islands of Ios and Anafi. In Greek, Santorini is also known as Thira or Thera. Santorini is a part of the Cycladic group of Islands. The area of the Island is 96 sq km whereas the coastline surrounding the Island stretches for almost 69 km. The capital of Santorini is Fira and the entire population of the Island is about 13,500 people. The main port of the Island is Athinios and it gets extremely busy in the summer months. This Island has always been subjected to volcanic eruptions from ancient time's right up to the modern era. When you arrive on the Island of Santorini just one look at the giant Caldera and the impressive geology of Santorini Island reveals to you the dreadful volcanic activity that has taken place here in the past so tread lightly to not disturb the sleeping giant!…

The Island of **Santorini**

Exploring the Island of Santorini

The best example of the geography of the Island of Santorini is the famous caldera that has played the major role in the history of the Island. The caldera is circular in shape and is entirely filled with sea water. In fact, it is the only sunken caldera in the world. It resembles a lagoon as the water depth here is only 400 meters. The caldera is surrounded by gigantic cliffs on top of which beautiful villages have been built. According to geologists, the first known eruption took place here in the year 1,645 BC. This eruption was responsible for the high tsunami waves that hit the northern coast of the Island of Crete and destroyed the fabulous Minoan civilisation that flourished there and on the Island of Santorini itself at that time…

The Island of Santorini

Exploring the Island of Santorini

It has also been speculated that the seismic activity of the Santorini volcano could be an explanation for the Exodus of Moses and the Jews from Egypt. For almost 1300 years after the eruption of 1,645 BC, the volcano was completely inactive. It eventually started having minor eruptions which led to the creation of the Islands of Palea Kameni, Mikra Kameni, Macronisi, Aspronisi and Nea Kameni. The last serious eruption happened as recently as 1957, when the earthquake destroyed many houses and public buildings on the Island. Since then, the volcano of Santorini has been monitored by scientists and geologists monitoring the seismic activity so they can give early warning of the potential for future eruptions to the Islanders…

The Island of **Santorini**

Exploring the Island of Santorini

The extreme volcanic activity, over the years, has formed the culture and architecture of the Island. The villages of Santorini are perched on the edge of the caldera and give breathtaking views out to sea. I can remember, as if it was only yesterday, just standing on the top of these cliffs, for a long time, just marvelling at the beauty and magnificence of the view before me. Having taken in the superb views it was time for us to visit the long hidden buried treasure on the Island that is the **Archeological Wonderland of the Minoan site at Akrotiri** …

The Island of Santorini

Volcanic Beach…

Akrotiri…

Exploring the Island of Santorini

The World famous archaeological site of **Akrotiri** is one of the main attractions of the Island of Santorini. Located on the southern side of the Island, between the village of Akrotiri and the famous red beach, this site is visited by thousands of visitors every year. Excavations on Akrotiri was started as early as the 1870's by the French Archaeological School of Athens. Few years later in 1866, the first traces of an ancient settlement had been revealed, during the work that was being done to get volcanic soil from the Island of Santorini and transport it in order to be used to insulate the Suez Canal Bridge. In the century that followed, many excavations were conducted. The famous archaeologist Spyridon Marinatos started excavating the site in 1967. As we entered the site we were very much looking forward to seeing for ourselves all the well preserved Minoan remains found on this site…

The Island of Santorini

Exploring the Island of Santorini

The work of the archaeologist Spyridon Marinatos and his team revealed a fully-working and developed settlement on the Akrotiri site (see above). The archaeologists concluded that the town they had uncovered was originally constructed around 4,500 B.C. but in the 17th century B.C. It was destroyed by an earthquake. A new town was built on the ruins of the old town, until it was also destroyed by another volcanic eruption about one century later…

The Island of Santorini

Exploring the Island of Santorini

At Akrotiri the archaeologists worked very hard and unearthed the location of a Minoan Town. They discovered that it was ideally located and served as a safe port which therefore, made it an important trading centre. The Towns urban planning was of densely packed houses, the buildings had two floors or more and there walls had been decorated with many amazing frescoes. The streets of the Town were paved and there were also open squares and storehouses. The wall frescoes depict a rich society, where people were dressed luxuriously and elegantly…

The Island of Santorini

Exploring the Island of Santorini

The evidence suggests that the enormous volcanic eruption that destroyed the settlement at Akrotiri took place in around 1,650 B.C. The entire Town was covered with a thick layer of volcanic ash and lava that helped to preserved Akrotiri almost intact for the next 3,666 years! As no human bodies have ever been found covered by ash or lava in the Town, as is the case in Pompeii, archaeologists believe that precursory earthquakes warned the residence of the impending catastrophe which gave them the chance to leave before the volcano erupted. Also not many valuable items were excavated from the site, which shows that between the earthquakes and the big volcanic eruption, the residents had returned to take their personal belongings. This time interval between the precursory earthquakes and the eruption has been estimated at about 10 days. The time between the first eruptions and the geological formation of the caldera has been estimated at being no more than 2-3 days. The eruption took place probably in spring because flowers of olive trees were found under the lava ashes. This was the most important eruption in the world for the last 10,000 years and the tsunami waves that raised also destroyed the Minoan Town of Knossos and much, much more on the Island of Crete…

The Island of Santorini

Exploring the Island of Santorini

In summary: The crescent-shaped Island of Santorini (or Thíra), the precious gem of the Aegean, is actually a group of Islands consisting of Thíra, Thirassiá, Asproníssi, Palea and Nea Kaméni in the southernmost part of Cyclades group of Islands. The whole complex of Santorini Islands is still an **Active Volcano** (the same as Méthana, Mílos and Nísiros) and probably the only volcano in the world whose crater is in the sea? The Islands that form Santorini came into existence as a result of intensive volcanic activity; twelve huge eruptions occurred, one every 20,000 years approximately, and each violent eruption caused the collapse of the volcano's central part creating a large crater (caldera). The volcano, however, has always managed to recreate itself over and over again. Ready to cause havoc and mass destruction once again…

The Island of **Santorini**

Exploring the Island of Santorini

The last really big eruption on Santorini occurred 3,666 years ago (during the great Minoan Age), when igneous material (mainly ash, pumice and lava stones) covered the three Islands (Thíra, Thirassiá and Asproníssi). On Santorini the eruption destroyed the thriving local prehistoric Minoan civilisation, evidence of which was found during the excavations of a settlement at Akrotiri. The solid material and gases emerging from the volcano's interior created a huge "vacuum" underneath, causing the collapse of the central part of the volcano and the creation of an enormous "pot" today's Caldera. The caldera that was left had a size of 8 x 4 km and a depth of up to 400 m below sea level. In the relatively recent history of the area the eruption of the submarine volcano Kolúmbo which is located 6.5 km. NE of the Island of Santorini, on 27th September 1650, was actually the largest eruption that has been recorded in the Eastern Mediterranean during the past millennium! The most recent volcanic activity on the Island itself occurred in 1950. The whole Island is actually a huge natural geological/volcano-logical museum where a wide range of geological structures and forms can be seen. As we boarded our boat after seeing all that we could of Santorini and set sail once again for the Island of Crete. It had been a very long day out. We had marveled at the views from the cliffs, walked on a volcanic Island, rested on a red beach, walk in the footsteps of the Minoans in the ancient town of Akrotiri and learnt about these amazing people. It was now time to leave the Island of Santorini. We had enjoyed our visit to the Island of Santorini but we were ready to get back to our resort to continue enjoying the sun, sand and sea for the rest of our holiday on the beautiful Island of Crete. Just before we come to the end of our adventure together there is just time, in the last chapter for us to enjoy seeing some of the best images of **The Island of Santorini in Colour**…

Santorini in Colour

The beautiful Island of Santorini

Santorini in Colour

The beautiful Island of Santorini

Santorini in Colour

The beautiful Island of Santorini

Santorini in Colour

The beautiful Island of Santorini

Santorini in Colour

The beautiful Island of Santorini

Santorini in Colour

The beautiful Island of Santorini

Santorini in Colour

The beautiful Island of Santorini

Santorini in Colour

The beautiful Island of Santorini

Santorini in Colour

The beautiful Island of Santorini

Santorini in Colour

Now that we have seen all the beauty and colour of these two wonderful Islands it is time for us to say farewell. As I wave you a fond goodbye I hope that you have enjoyed our time together and so until the next time, be happy and keep well. I hope that you have a great Greek summer holiday real soon…

Acknowledgement

I would like to thank all the people of the Greek Islands of Crete and Santorini that we met during our holiday on their beautiful Islands. I would also like to thank my publishers Rainbow Publications UK. For publishing this book and for giving me the opportunity for my books to be read once more. Finally I wish to thank my wife Susie for her love and support that she gives me, in all that I do, every single day of my life.

Susie… 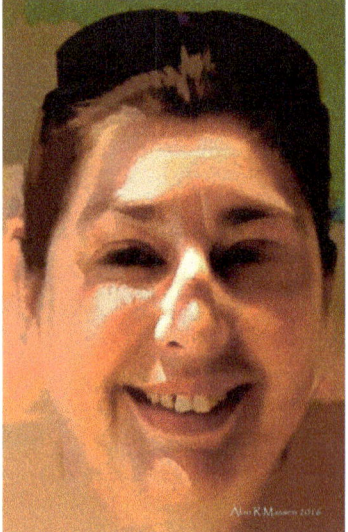  **…Alan**

Copyright © 2020 Alan R. Massen

I wish you all a very big
Thank You

www.ingramcontent.com/pod-product-compliance
Lightning Source LLC
Chambersburg PA
CBHW061926290426
44113CB00024B/2830